My Strength Comes From Within

by Joye M. Carter, M.D.

Biblical Dogs™

My Strength Comes From Within

An Inspirational Thought Package.
Learn How, With Dedication and Self
Discipline,
To Follow Your Dream and
Achieve Success in Your Career.

by Joye M. Carter, M.D.

My Strength Comes From Within

Publisher's Cataloging-in-Publication
(Provided by Quality Books, Inc.)

Carter, Joye M.
    My strength comes from within / by Joye M. Carter. --
1st ed.
    p. cm.
    Includes index.
    LCCN 00-192152
    ISBN 0-9703722-6-4

    1. Carter, Joye M. 2. Medical examiners (Law)—
United States—Biography. 3. Afro-American Physicians—
United States—Biography. 4. Premedical education—
United States—Biography. 5. Medical students—United
States—Biography. 6. Medical colleges—United States—
Admission.   I. Title

RA1025.C37A3 2000   614.1'092
                    QBI00-901537

Printed in the United States of America
Printed on acid free paper

Biblical Dogs™
Houston, Texas

Cover design by Volume Media, Inc.
Photographs by Provost Studios

Dedication

In loving memory of

Momma Hart, Daddy, Special K and

Sable

This book is dedicated to all little girls who are just
a little different
and to dog lovers everywhere.

Acknowledgements

To the Lord above for giving me the patience, persistence, wisdom, and ability to use my talents to benefit others. I am truly blessed, but only by His choosing!

To my Mom for insisting I learn well.

To my sister, Sharon, for her help and encouragement.

To Judy for her tireless fingers and always excellent assistance.

To Melanie for her wonderful editing.

To Mack and Sara for their invaluable assistance and support.

To Kirk and Barbara at Studio 21 for keeping my head together.

To Walter for his support during these trying times.

To all my friends for helping me when I needed it the most.

To Samson and Delila for welcoming me home each day with unconditional love.

Contents

◆

Preface

"Dr. Carter's autobiography, of a young person aspiring to reach her dreams, is unquestionably needed. It provides an insightful and well-written look at an inspiring and emotional journey. Today's youth need role models who are willing to share their challenges and modes of coping. Dr. Carter's life lessons are especially significant for young blacks and women. She is a shining example of someone who set goals, developed a plan, and achieved.

The fact that Dr. Carter was endowed with the confidence to pursue her goals and remain steadfast against her opponents, both personally and professionally, has caused the "old guard" to become noticeably baffled by the young people who dare to pursue excellence. Dr. Carter identifies a period in American history when those who were previously left out earned the right to take their place in pursuit of the "American Dream."

Dr. Carter's autobiography should be required reading for all those at risk for letting the 'establishment' direct their life course."

Edith Irby Jones, M.D.
First black female to be President of the National Medical Association and the first person of color to attend medical school in the state of Arkansas (under guard)

Foreword

"This book gives America a glimpse of what makes this nation great. In a society still dominated by males, a society where, as General Colin Powell proclaims, "race is still a barrier to success, Dr. Joye M. Carter has achieved so much at such a young age. Her drive to do well in whatever she attempts, her tenacious clinging to values she learned in her close-knit family, her demands on herself to stay the course whatever the obstacles – these attributes and more are laid out for us in this remarkable book. She might have asked a highly esteemed medical professional to write a foreword. She certainly might have been expected to ask a strong woman who has fought the battles of sexism and racism to write it. Instead, she asked her pastor, a male himself, often guilty of chauvinist attitudes, to write it. This brilliant and tough young woman, the first black female chief medical examiner in the United States, who at thirty-four was named chief medical examiner for Washington, D.C., asked her pastor, because, in her own words, "I believe all that I have achieved and overcome is a result of a close relationship with God."

What profound wisdom in a high achiever who might credit her own brilliance to her lofty position!

This is a book that ought to be read by those who have been unsuccessful in their attempts to achieve their goals, as well as by powerful insiders. It ought to be read by the elderly and by children. It certainly needs to be read by anybody who feels they are limited by external circumstance. Dr. Joye Carter, Chief Medical Examiner for Harris County, Texas, is an incredible blend of medical acumen, spiritual depth, toughness under fire, and gentleness with underdogs. This attractive, young woman, sufficiently honest to give her age in this book, is a natural role model for girls, especially minority girls, who need to know that they can achieve their goals.

You will see in these thirty-one conversational "thought-packages" (not so much chapters as personal soliloquies), the pithy, cut-to-the-chase personality that brings out the best of warm family origins in Wellsville, Ohio; the crux of wise and effective teachers from elementary school to medical school; the mentoring of Dade County's Chief Medical Examiner, Dr. Joseph H. Davis; the sparks of wisdom from grass-roots people; and the assurance that God was with her every step of the way. You will understand her indomitable spirit in Chapter Two, especially the eloquent poem, "Woman in Charge."

Dr. Carter has bared her soul to her invisible audience. This bright and beautiful woman makes it plain in her reflections why she has revolutionized the office of the Chief Medical Examiner in Harris County, and why she is so embattled in the county which sends more human beings to the death chamber than any other in the nation. You can hear in her literary dialogue with the reader the sage teachings of her maternal grandmother, the "can-do" attitude of her professional mentor, Dr. Joseph Davis, and the unflagging faith in the God of Moses: "who shall overcome any obstacle with only a servant who will obey His will."

15

Don't be surprised if you can't put it down."

Reverend William H. Lawson

Pastor of Wheeler Avenue

Baptist Church

Houston, Texas, 2000

My Strength Comes From Within

The autobiography of Joye M. Carter, M.D.,
first black female to become a chief medical
examiner in the United States

♦ *My Strength Comes From Within* ♦

Who Am I?

I am Joye Maureen Carter, the youngest of four daughters born to Russell and Marjorie Carter in the very small town of Wellsville, Ohio. I was born in 1957. People always ask me, "Why do you include the year you were born? Don't you know women don't like to tell their age?"

As you come to know me, you will learn that I speak my mind, and I am proud to be the age I am now - 43. I think it is important that we as women abandon the old adage that the older we get, the less productive and important we are to society. So I abandoned that notion. I am 43! I have gray hair; I've earned every one, earned them the right way. I am very proud of the fact that I grayed early, in my twenties, and take after my mother's side of the family. I'm not shy about my age.

Like most of you, I am multi-dimensional. In fact, I consider myself a tapestry woven of all the different experiences I will discuss in this book. I don't think I fit into any one category. I call myself a black woman, not because it is politically correct, but because I feel comfortable describing myself that way. Many years ago when I was very small, I learned that my grandmother used the word "colored," my father used the word "black," and the struggle for me was coming around. Deciding what to call yourself is learning how to be comfortable with who you are. They use the word "white" people, but I've never seen a "white" person; they are really kind of pink and tan. They use the word "black," but I've never really seen a "black" person. I have seen all different hues.

I would like to share a real life story that I have spoken about many, many times. At about the time I was reaching puberty, I was struggling with my identity. We were still living in the small town in Ohio, and my parents moved to the next small town with a whopping population of 25,000. That was East Liverpool. I was the only person of color in my fifth grade class. At that time, I was going through a growth spurt. I was tall for my age with large feet, and I was very uncomfortable. But I had always been a good student and excelled in school, and I loved to read. My white classmates didn't really appreciate that I actually was very smart and earned good grades. I remember suffering dearly every time the test scores came out. At one point, I figured that my fifth grade teacher really liked me. She used to talk to me, show off my papers, and kind of brag about what I was doing in class. But one day that changed. I recall this as a pivotal point in my development.

One fall day, I was sitting in the classroom, and we were discussing world history. All of a sudden, I was singled out by Ms. McBurney. She pointed to me and her words burned into my very soul. "Joye can stay out longer in the sun because her skin is dark and her ancestors came from Africa." This summed up this teacher's introductory lecture on the great continent of Africa.

Suddenly I was the center of attention in that fifth grade classroom. My heart had dropped through my feet, and my classmates stared at me. Not only did I look different, but I felt completely different. People were staring at me as if I was not a human being. I was mortified. I was embarrased. I was angry. I closed my eyes for what was probably only a couple of seconds but seemed like a lifetime and I prayed. *"God, please open this floor and swallow me; I don't want to be different. I want to be just like them."*

In my little, tiny soul, my heart was so hurt, and I was so embarrassed. I was also angry because I was brown and had kinky hair. But those feelings didn't last for long. While I had my head bowed, I opened my eyes a little bit and discovered that there was no hole I could slip through into the floor. It just didn't work that way. So my mind kicked into high gear and a thought occurred to me. During that brief second of emotional embarrassment in that fifth grade classroom, my mind clicked over and recalled something I had read in *Ebony* magazine. It was an article on skin cancer. As that thought churned in my mind, I perked up. I lifted my head from my desk, opened my eyes, and looked around.

Then I stood up and I said, "Ms. McBurney, you're right. I can stay outside longer because my ancestors are from Africa. My ancestors are also from the United States, the first Americans, and I remember reading that I can stay out longer but I won't have the same risk of skin cancer. I read that in *Ebony* magazine. I can stay out longer because my ancestors' skin is better protected against skin cancer. They are doing skin cancer research at Howard University." Then I said, "May I be excused." I got up, put my hands on what was in my imagination, and walked out of the room to the principal's office and said, "May I please use the phone to call my mother?"

Well, I called my mother. She was teaching in another town, and, at that time, I was crying. I was hurt, but I was also feeling stronger, and, at that point, I said to myself, *You have something to be proud of.* Oh, the power of education! That indeed was a pivotal point in my life. I learned then that I would never, ever be embarrassed about my ethnic background again. That there was something valuable in me, and I vowed never to covet any other physical characteristics of anybody. That's a lot to learn when in fifth grade. It was a very powerful lesson.

Getting back to my mother: When I told her what had happened, she, of course, called my teacher, and being a teacher herself, volunteered to teach my teacher about slavery.

I say this to young people: It wasn't that in my fifth grade I began to hate. In fifth grade, I learned to accept my background and to be proud of who I am. That was a turning point. I honestly cannot recall another time when I bowed my head, except to worship God, and I'm proud of that now. That encouraged me to learn more.

Looking back as an adult now, it has paid off for me. If you have learned anything about me by this point, remember, *No matter where you come from, no matter who you are, there is something special about you that needs to be celebrated.*

What Does Growing Into Blackness Mean?

I guess it wasn't easy for my sisters to deal with me. I guess I was really a little strange, if you want to call it that. I loved school and hated to miss a day. I think it was because I was an avid reader, and when I read, I was transformed and transported to another place. I think my favorite books, when I was a little girl, were books about mythology, fairy tales, and the heroes' books. What were heroes' books? The children's section of our small town library had these beautiful books about all the people we learned about in history, but these books discussed their lives as young people. I read about George Washington, Washington Carver, all the different presidents, and I enjoyed the stories about their youths. How exciting! Not only were they exciting, but they showed a side of these people as young men and women. The books showed these famous persons getting into mischief and trouble while growing up, and I realized that everybody starts somewhere. People aren't born famous. Certainly, some people are born noteworthy, but they have a development period. I began to really believe that I was going to be okay, that I could develop into a "shero" or anything else I wanted to be. That came from reading!

If I can say one word to you . . READ! We must learn to read. We have got to learn to read with a discerning eye. We have got to learn to question what we read. We have to learn to read everything. For me, the biggest development in world history was the printing press because all of a sudden people could read for themselves. Many educated people didn't want to share that knowledge and pass it on. As a young girl, I was a deep thinker. I developed critical thought as a young person. Some people referred to it as "sass." I just knew I had the right to question some things. Not flippantly but I really wanted to know why. As a young girl, I would lose myself for hours in a book. My sisters really didn't understand their wacky little sister; that was okay because I grew into it.

I began this section talking about what it means to "grow into blackness." I describe myself as black. I don't usually use the term "African American." To me it's just too wordy, and again, it's a choice. I don't condemn one over the other. But there is another reason I call myself black.

I was in a very small town with a very small number of black people. In fact, almost every black person in this small town was related to me. After all, my father had fourteen brothers and sisters. Despite growing up in Ohio, I found that I was linked to the outside world (music was important to me). My hero of the day was James Brown, the Godfather of Soul! He would put a record out, it seemed like almost every week, and I would save my pennies that I earned from selling soda pop bottles and running errands to buy another record. I don't recall what age I was, but I remember James Brown reaching out to touch me in my formative years. The record "Say it Loud, I'm Black and I'm Proud" was *the* song, and I must admit that today, as a forty-something year old, oh yeah, I can shake it with that record on. That's my theme song, and when I need to get up and go in the morning, hey, I'm struttin' it to James Brown!

That song reaches out to me again as an individual, and I love it!! It has stuck with me all these years .. . "Say it Loud, I'm Black and I'm Proud!" It says it all! It doesn't say "Say it Loud, I'm Black and I'm Better Than Anybody." It just says, "Say it Loud, I'm Black and I'm Proud." I hope all of you reading this will say, "Hey, whatever I am, I'm proud of it." To date, I don't know of any person on this earth who asked to be born. So you've got to make the most of who you are. Live with it. That's what I say.

As a young black female, I struggled early on with not only how I felt about myself but with my physical characteristics. My three older sisters looked a bit more like my mother's side of the family than I thought I did. I didn't think that was fair then, but, it kind of evened out over time. I learned a long time ago to accept myself the way I am, but it was hard. As a young girl I was skinny, like a zipper, with huge, round, brown eyes. If you recall the old fairy tale about the dog with eyes like saucers, well, that was me. My sisters and others always teased me about the size of my eyes. I had to grow into them. I also ended up with what I call the fullest lips. I remember the cruelty of some of my classmates talking about my full lips that they called "liver lips." But we all know how cruel kids can sometimes be. I also grew into this too.

On the following page is a poem that I wrote about appreciating my beautiful characteristics and shielding myself from the ignorant comments that I received. This poem describes so many of my experiences, as well as my feelings. I would like to share it with you now.

Woman In Charge

Men see me coming and they stop and pause;

one brave soul politely asks how I got in charge.

I smile sweetly and take no offense,

because living well is a benefit of common sense.

Some stare, some moan, some stand in awe;

they know deep inside its not the effect of the Wonder Bra.

You see, my mind is tough. My thoughts are unique;

be mentally alert with me or face verbal defeat.

My hands are blessed, for I serve a cause.

Stand back, Fellas! It's not menopause.

My words are firm but full of tact,

because in the end I just record the facts.

A man may acquire material things it's true,

but after death we remember the things that you do.

A kind word, a gentle touch, concern for a fellow man

does a whole lot more than diamonds covering one's hand.

At this point you think I am wise beyond my years,

because I have witnessed so many other's tears.

Most people believe I won the right to be the woman in charge;

my hope is that we all end up on the same heaven bound barge.

The way I perceive myself comes from early exposure to a variety of beautiful people of all different hues in the *Ebony* and *Jet* magazines. It was rare at that time to see brown women on television. Seeing these women meant a lot to me, and there were not enough of them. Black women with full lips and natural hairstyles were becoming popular, as were their broad hips. Oh, I just knew I was going to be sassy!

It helped to have nurturing words from my grandmother saying, "There is no one on this earth better than you. There is no one on this earth more beautiful than you. And, at the same time, you are no better than anyone else on this earth."

She taught me to recognize that things could always be different, could always be worse. You talk about having thick lips. What if you didn't have any lips? What if your mouth was scarred, and you couldn't open it to talk or laugh or even eat? Things could always be worse. Be proud. Be glad of what you have. Those are the words that I live by.

How Did You Keep Your Dream Alive
In High School and College?

A question that I am frequently asked when giving a presentation is "What is my educational background?" Although I mentioned my education in the previous chapter, I want to reiterate again for the sake of any young person reading this and asking, "Hey, is it ever too late?" Usually, it's not, but I want you to be prepared as early as you can for your chosen career.

In high school, I really wanted to do two things. I wanted to be a bio-engineer and a physician. My high school years are not the ones I look back on with the most fondness. High school, for me, was a little difficult because I was one of those kids who was just too . . . too . . . too . . . brainy. I was too obedient. I was too thin. I spoke too white. I was not too popular.

Now, for all those young people who didn't quite fit in, this one's for you. I knew in my heart I wasn't going to be in high school forever. I had a knack for finding people similar to, and yet a little different from, to become friends with and to grow with. The friends I made in high school are still my friends today. I took up their good points and left the negative ones there. It's a talent that I acquired as a child. I was comfortable enough with myself. I didn't need to be the most popular one; I already possessed self-confidence and an unexpected level of maturity for my age. I was a "do-gooder," a "smart one," a "brainiac." While these terms are not negative, they were not always flattering to me as a teenager, especially when coming from my peer group. As a young girl I was considered a "goody two-shoes." Fear of parents, grandparents, and God will make you earn labels like this. But I managed.

I was very fortunate to be exposed to a variety of interests such as the arts, science, and culture as a young girl. I was already a model of diversity.

I had been exposed through reading to different writers and genres. I acquired a love of the J.R.R.Tolkien literature, as well as my favorite short story author, Edgar Allan Poe. Boy, was I creepy! In fact, my nickname was "blood and pus." People knew I liked scary stories by Edgar Allan Poe and the actor, Vincent Price. I enjoyed good quality, thrilling movies, not "how to kill a teenager twenty-five ways," but things that made me think about the "possible."

I also loved music. I grew up in the Midwest and developed an appetite for many different types of music, which I maintain to date. I'm musically diverse, growing up with a little country western, a lot of rock-n-roll, soul music, gospel, classical, and opera. I was lucky to go to a public high school that offered exposure in this area. I am a very proud product of public education, as well as home schooling. I developed a love for dance and was able to study various forms in high school. I sang with a group from high school and performed for many occasions around Indianapolis.

As a small child in Ohio, I was ill. I had developed measles twice. The first set of vaccinations in the early sixties didn't take with me, so I developed measles a second time and almost died. I was bedridden for a while with a very high fever and something called measle encephalitis where the outer lining of my brain was infected, and I wasn't supposed to live. But I did. When I was beginning to recover, I had a problem with my balance. I began to study dance shortly after becoming well again and acquired a love for motion. So I developed into a student with a voracious appetite for learning whatever I could. Because of this knowledge and also with my strong stubborn streak, which I had to learn to quell a little bit, I did become a leader among some of my classmates in high school. I was involved with student government and biology. Through these arenas, I continued to do well in academics, a rewarding feat.

Now, one thing I have to confess again, I fully admit to being stubborn, and I had already made up my mind that I wanted to be a doctor, but I encountered a problem. In high school, I had a guidance counselor, I don't remember his name, I think it was Mr. Davis. When I told him I had plans to become a physician, he wasn't supportive. He kind of laughed at me. He said, "Ah, medicine is not for you."

I could have accepted that, but I said, "Oh, no, I don't think you're the one to tell me that medicine is not for me. You are supposed to be a guidance counselor. Why would you try to dash my dreams?" I believed in myself enough to go to the principal and say, "I want another counselor, one to guide me, not stop me." But they wouldn't give me another guidance counselor, and I wasn't going to make a big deal of it; after all, I was just a high school student.

Along the way, I made friends with an older woman named Mrs. Green. Mrs. Green was a black woman, a counselor at Shortridge, frail in body but strong in character and she said, "Baby, you can be anything you prepare yourself to be." She is the one who led me on the pathway to get that first job in the hospital. "A foot in the door," she had said, "is all you need." I still remember those words today. But it didn't stop there. I excelled in my classes. That didn't mean, however, that I was always going to succeed. I remember being so pleased to have a Ph.D. level chemistry teacher, Mrs. Vanhorn. She was one of the first women, she was white, to receive her Doctorate in biochemistry from Harvard, and she was an excellent instructor. I did very well in her course, and I remember her asking the students what we wanted to be. I said I wanted to be a doctor.

One day I was doing a special project with her. "Woman to woman," she said, "Oh, you'll get into medical school because you're black, female, and you're kind of cute." Boy, was I angry! What did she say that for?

I said, "No, Mrs. Van Horn, I'll get into medical school because I'm qualified." I always had to make sure that people knew that I was confident in my abilities and that my abilities lived up to my expectations because I felt that other people's expectations were too low. So to my readers now, please, don't forget: you have to live with yourself. Back it up; back your words up with some actions!

When I began applying to college however, I had to make a choice. I really had my sights set on one of the very large universities in Indiana because I wanted to stay with my friends. I wanted to go where it was cheaper, and I knew I had the benefit of a good education in Indiana. That didn't last long because I began to go on interviews with my mother and soon found myself interested in the small private colleges in Ohio. Wittenberg University seemed particularly attractive to me. I had fallen in love with the campus. It was a somewhat exclusive, private institution with a very high tuition. The school had offered me an academic scholarship, so those good grades paid off. The main reason I wanted to go to Wittenberg was because it had an excellent reputation for pre-law, pre-business, and pre-medical studies. They also had a wonderful language/arts department, which taught Greek. I wanted to study the Greek language. I had already studied Latin for the previous eight years and I took it because I decided I wanted to become a doctor early on.

I ended up at Wittenberg University, a small, private, Lutheran school located in Springfield, Ohio. The university rests in a beautiful pastoral setting with old red brick buildings and ivy, the whole bit, in a very small town with very little to distract from my studies. Initially, I had some regrets about going to Wittenberg since I really missed my friends. They had all started school so much earlier. In Indiana, most colleges begin in August, but as a Wittenberg student, I had to wait until September, so I felt a little cheated. When I got to Wittenberg, I was surprised to learn that, in spite of a full four-year academic scholarship which included the tuition, my room and board and all other expenses and supplies, it was too expensive. I had a difficult time coping, and I ended up working three jobs to be able to afford all the things outside the tuition. I worked as a laboratory assistant the whole time I was at Wittenberg. I worked as a tutorer, and I worked as a manager in the student center. I found it easy to get involved at Wittenberg for a couple of strange reasons. Number one, I was a good student. I enjoyed the science department. On the other hand, there were so few black students in my department that it was a little difficult to get the proper guidance that I felt I needed. There were no black professors in the health sciences whatsoever. So I had to look elsewhere for a mentor. In fact, there were only two black faculty members the whole time I was at Wittenberg. Finding someone who really cared about me as a person was hard. I did manage to locate a black female professor in another department, and I latched on to her quickly.

Wittenberg's population was mostly white, less than two percent black. For a small, private, Lutheran school, whose main focus was academics, it had excellent sports. Wittenberg, like many other schools at that time in the late seventies, would bring in black student athletes from all over the country, those who didn't make the cuts at the Big Ten schools. So they had excellent football and basketball teams. Many of the black athletes who would come in had not really made the academic requirements, and while they were there, they enjoyed their popularity and were often given spending money for weekends. But Wittenberg was very strict. If you didn't meet a certain grade cut, you did not graduate. Many young black men came to Wittenberg and played their hearts out, but that was it. End of story. By the time they were either put on academic probation or at the point of graduation, they didn't have the credits, and they didn't get that piece of paper. I tried to influence the students coming in behind me to be careful of that. I worked in earnest as a tutor.

Funny, but then the tide turned. At Wittenberg, my main focus was to graduate and go to medical school. I was chastised so many times by some of my black colleagues for not being black enough. What did that mean? Well, the one thing I absolutely refused to do was sit in the black section of the cafeteria where many of the minority students would gather. It was segregation, nothing more! I was chastised for not partying and skipping class, for not smoking and drinking, and for not hanging out. Of course, this activity is common to all ethnic groups in college. I was told I didn't sound black enough, and I had a very unpleasant nickname. That was kind of tough because I was already being singled out in the Science Department. But again, I knew that this was a temporary situation, and I was going to get out of there soon. I must say, the main people who chided me for the sound of my voice, who mocked me for going to class and for not hanging out, were the same ones I left behind when I got my diploma. Sad to say!

While the black students did not see me as black enough or enough of a partier, the white administration saw me as the poster child for affirmative action. Whenever they needed to demonstrate that they had top black scholars at the school, they called me. Whenever they needed someone to sit on a panel to discuss relationships between black and white students, they called me. I became a "wonder child." It was really kind of hard to take after a while. I got fed up because I didn't feel like anybody cared about *me* and what *I* wanted.

At the same time, while I was excelling in my classes, there was a very strong reluctance on the part of my pre-med counselor to give me what I needed to matriculate into medical school. I needed a Dean's letter stating that I was qualified and academically prepared to accept the challenge of medical school. So here I was at the top of my class, studying hard every day, working three jobs, and this one professor, I will never forget his name, Dr. Bolls, said to me that he didn't think I would do well in medical school. Now this had happened to another black student a year ahead of me and that person had given up, but I, being the fighter that I was, wasn't accepting that. My question was, "What makes you think I am not going to do well in medical school?" He didn't have a reason to give me; he just didn't think so. He also didn't think I was going to *get* into medical school. And, again, my question to him was "Why? Why are you denying me an opportunity? My grades are good; I'm involved in all kinds of student activities. What is it?" For almost six months, I had to fight to get a dean's letter. When I got the Dean's letter from Wittenberg, it was the most lukewarm, non-exciting letter anybody could have written.

It essentially said, *Hey, if you want to take a chance on her, go right ahead.* I was really unhappy! I thought for awhile, and I could have made a tremendous fuss, which I started to do, but I felt like it was a waste of my time to give my energy to negative people. So I took the letter that I received from the biology department, and I put it with a letter that I wrote about myself, my aspirations, my goals to become a medical examiner, and then I sent it to several different medical schools. Instead of having an angry attitude, I buckled down and studied more. I took and passed the MCAT, the medical college examination, and I did quite well. When I received a little thin envelope in the mail I discovered that I had been accepted to *seven* medical schools. I didn't even bother to mention it to my uninformed counselor. I just let it speak for itself. That was another turning point in my life because I had watched people who came before and after me get discouraged by the attitude at Wittenberg, and I saw their dreams drop by the wayside.

There was another incident that occurred at Wittenberg that changed my mind about my career plans. Initially, I had wanted to go back to Indiana. In fact, I had already secured a place at Indiana University which was notorious for not being kind to black medical students. I wanted to go home, and I wanted to save money because, again, I wasn't really thinking about securing finances. Getting into medical school was one thing, funding it was another. An incident occurred at Wittenberg where there was some name calling and physical contact, and a shooting took place. A black student shot a white student, and racial tensions soared. After that, I made up my mind to forego going to Indiana University and to seek out one of my earlier goals which was to go to Howard University where I would have role models who looked like me. To be taught by the best and the brightest and to obtain reality-based, African-American disease health information were my main goals.

I had not applied to Meharry or Howard medical schools. But I was accepted. I guess the encoding on the MCAT that let them identify me as an African-American. I thought, *oh, well, I suppose I'm really tied into going to Indiana University.* Amazingly, some of my classmates from the Cincinnati area knew people who had gone to Howard, and I was instantly connected. I drove up to Howard University one weekend and while there I learned about real generosity. A friend of a friend's father knew a dentist in Baltimore. I don't remember the dentist's name but I went to Baltimore with this classmate of mine who I didn't know well until the trip. But we drove together to Baltimore and stayed the night at the home of a dentist who had also gone to the dental school at Howard University.

This gentleman was elderly, probably in his sixties, very kind, and I told him of my aspirations to become a medical examiner, a forensic pathologist. He was very encouraging. He took me to his office in the central, inner city of Baltimore where he had restored an old building in the low income area. He had a very large practice which he would hand over to a younger professional upon retirement. He hadn't met me before, knew nothing about my family, or me for that matter, but he trusted me. The next morning when I woke up, I was to drive into Washington, D.C. and have an interview. He came up to me and presented me with the keys to his wife's Mercedes Benz, a 450 SLC, the car I had salivated over in high school. He said, "You go and do a good job and make us proud." Can you imagine me driving into the city in this beautiful car?

I said, "But you know nothing about me. How can I repay your generosity?"

You know what he said to me? He said, "You can repay me by going to school, finishing it, and completing your goal."

Well, I can tell you one thing. I went to that interview and I said, "I'm the one you need in this class, even though I'm late." And I was accepted.

People back at Wittenberg asked me, "What made you decide to go to Howard?"

I said, "Because it's a black school, and I feel the need now to go where people have my interests at heart and I can learn." Was that the end of it? Not really. It's amazing, but when I said I was going to go to Howard for medical school beyond Wittenberg, I didn't get a lot of the support I thought I would get at home. It was an issue. It was a sad issue that some of my relatives thought that Howard was not the best school for me to go to because it was black. I learned that people of my parents' generation had been led to believe that white was better than black. Some feared I would not reach my goals if I attended Howard.

Having experienced Wittenberg, I felt there was a good chance that black education would be what it should be, equal to, that of the white education. Even my family physician tried to talk me out of going to Howard. Well, of course I no longer needed a pediatrician, so what does that tell you? I remember very much my godparents, who by this time were just about to relocate to Houston, Texas. I remember telling my godmother that I was going to go to Howard, and she simply said to me, "We'll be there when you get out. You come see us now." That was all the encouragement I needed. I was on my way to Howard.

What Was It Like At Howard?

Howard was a trip, an end unto itself! It seemed like I had tried most of my life to get to this university. I was so excited to be a medical student and a young military officer. I was also naïve. I found out that one of my high school classmates, Lucia, a very good friend who had gone to college in Indiana, was going to Howard for medical school. We decided to room together. In fact, we had planned a whole wonderful summer. We were going to go to Washington, pick out an apartment, and then we were going to travel to Europe. Both of us drove to Howard in my girlfriend's car to look for a place to live. We didn't have a lot of money. She also was in the military, but she had gotten a Navy scholarship. I will never forget pulling up on Fourteenth Street, right around Howard University, and someone running up to the car and saying, "Hey, you want to buy some gold?"

We looked at each other and said, "No, we don't need any jewelry, thank you." We thought we knew it all! The man was talking about marijuana! We had no idea because we didn't use drugs. But what an education we got in Washington,

D.C., an education about health and about life. I transformed
from a Midwestern girl into a somewhat city-wise young lady.

When we got to Howard, Lucia and I felt a little bit
country. We had that kind of wholesome upbringing which I'm
so glad I had, looking back today. We were in a class of 120. It
was just so glorious watching the sea of different hues, from
creamy vanilla to deep, deep, ultra dark chocolate! Brilliant,
brilliant people from all over the world were in my class. So
much to learn, so many wonderful people, all kinds of attitudes,
all kinds of hair textures. It was just wonderful for me. But I
stuck out like a sore thumb. There were only six people out of
our class who were there on military scholarships, and the
question was always, "Why'd you do that; why would you want
to work for Uncle Sam?" Well, it was very simple for me. On
a military scholarship, my entire medical school expenses were
paid, and I was paid to go to school. I earned a $400 stipend a
month. Looking back now, I don't know how I managed to live
on $400 a month, but I sure did. I lived well on $400 a month.
I budgeted and saved my money and finally bought a car. It
seems impossible today, but I sure did it back then.

I was wearing my hair natural. People would say to me,
"Why?" There I was at Howard University, and I could count

the women in my entering class who had natural hair. People criticized me. People of color! I was criticized for not wearing the right clothes; I wasn't dressed snazzy enough! I ended up buying a Toyota. That wasn't fancy enough! I would tell them, "Look, I'm *in* medical school, not *out*. My priorities are a little bit different." What was the point? A lot of my classmates were there on other scholarships or there their parents' were paying or they took out tremendous loans. I was there to learn, not flaunt my money, so I wore jeans and T-shirts and studied lots. My classmates wore designer duds, but we had different priorities.

What I learned, lived, and saw at Howard was a harsh reality: some of us had not really learned our history. I found that many people of color around the Washington, D.C. area were so critical of other people of color. We were more caught up in characteristics and physique than other people. I heard the "N" word more than I could stand from people of color, and that was really sad. In fact, I thought it was quite pathetic.

I also noticed that a very strong degree of sexism existed at Howard. That was very disappointing. What happens to us as a people? Why do we buy into all of this false separatism?

Howard was an all-male-club in the late seventies into the early eighties. Many of the department chairs were good looking, light-complected black men with beautiful wives. There were fewer department heads who were of a hue deeper than coffee with cream. That was very disappointing. But every now and then I would meet someone, and I would kind of say to myself, "Now there is a person who has made it." It showed the need for education, for black folk to truly get educated. I received more criticism and questions from people of color than I did from others. For a while, it was very discouraging, though eventually, I found a little niche. There were people like me who had plans for the future and who weren't satisfied with the status quo.

While students at Howard, we invented the nickname "How Hard." For me, the first two years were relatively simple. I had all the pre-medical sciences as an undergrad, and I enjoyed a position in my medical school class of, well, basically being smart. I was able to relax a little bit and take advantage of my military career.

Now back to "How Hard." Why did we call it that? The third and fourth years of medical school are when doctors begin honing their skills, such as approaching the patient and talking to the patient. I felt so blessed to be at Howard because I had some excellent professors who made sure, if nothing else, I learned good, authentic bedside manner. I had a wonderful preceptor doctor. His name was Dr. Chisholm. He was actually from the Caribbean, and he loved his patients. I still credit him to this day for giving me the ability to establish rapport with patients. They didn't let me slide by with just anything. I had better know what I was talking about. I felt myself responding to this kind of teaching like a sponge, soaking it all in and wanting more.

There were a few professors at Howard who had come up through the military, had used the GI bill, had served in some of the wars, so they knew I was military, and they took me under their wing. They didn't cut me any slack, though. It was like this: "Young Dr. Carter, you're going to learn and learn it right." I enjoyed it. I enjoyed the discipline. I enjoyed the ability to talk to patients and figure out what was wrong with them. I must admit I did not enjoy the things that I had to do as a medical student. I honestly can't say that I believe one hundred percent in Western medicine philosophy. I think there is a very strong spiritual self-component to medicine. Patients have to believe in what's being done to them in order for medicine to work.

At Howard, I dedicated myself to my studies and attained my goals. I loved living in Washington, D.C., the "chocolate city." I loved being black, and for many years, I was starved for black culture, and now, there it was, in living color. One day I saw Sidney Poitier getting off the elevator at the hospital and I thought I was just going to scream my head off! The plays, the vibrant art, and all the different cultural centers in Washington, D.C., made it a wonderful place to live. I began to look at the art as a way of escape, of admiring beauty. I developed a love for black art in particular while in medical school. Though I couldn't afford it, I appreciated it. I was able to go to some of the plays, *For Colored Girls Who Have Contemplated Suicide When the Rainbow is Enuff,* and *The Piano Lesson,* and artists Nina Simone and Herbie Hancock. I experienced some of that culture, one on one, as a student. The majority of the black artists and entertainers, the theater, and jazz, were truly not supported by the black community, for these cultural events were too expensive for most black people.

I volunteered on my free Saturdays to work in the local high schools to mentor the students, and I realized some of the neighborhood high schools in Washington, D.C. were not preparing students for the future and for taking their college preparatory courses. It was really disheartening. I discovered a science book I had used in high school, some six years earlier, now outdated, but it was being used in the schools.

I began to learn that everything doesn't automatically become equal because you have an education. I decided to play an active role in politics, to learn what was going on, to be aware. It also seemed important to continue to read and learn as much as I could. It was kind of disappointing to learn that a lot of the "learned" people didn't get involved in politics, didn't vote, and didn't take part in that political process. Some people had forgotten, or maybe had not learned, that our forefathers had died to get us the right to vote. My colleagues and I kind of developed a core group of people who worked to get others out to the polls, to get involved, to learn, and to teach. Part of that experience was growing up and realizing that things aren't always the way I would have liked them to be.

Medical school was the best part of my education. That is the one place I return year after year for reunions or with the National Medical Association to keep my contacts. High school and college never reached that inner part of me. That period in

Washington was full of growth, vigorous training, and the ability to see the people I had only read about in *Ebony* and *Jet* magazines. For me, medical school was where I began maturing. I had found my niche! I met enough people like me who were brown and didn't speak the way everyone else did. Basically, I found people who weren't afraid to be themselves. That's what I learned about life while in medical school.

I also learned that I had the ability to touch patients. I learned in medical school that I had to go back to my home training and remember what I was taught as a little girl: to treat people with respect and to do it for myself. Those were principles that were so important. These ideals allowed me to move ahead. I was able to feel the patients' pain, to embrace those somewhat foreign medical concepts. Things I was taught as a little girl about principles, about respecting the elderly, about looking someone in the eye when I talked to them, became tools I could apply when learning those concepts. And that's what really helped me get through that process and earn my M.D. degree.

I gave a talk several years ago, ten years after finishing Howard, and I called the name of the talk "How Hard." I described the difficulty I had in making the transition from college as a small town Midwesterner to an urban medical school graduate. I said it was a growing process, a maturation process, a village-rearing process. I can say now with much pride: "Don't mess with me. I am a Howard Woman." And you know what? I mean every word.

How Did You Reach Your Goal?

I continued to work that summer, to read and do my research. I volunteered at the local police station in the small town where I went to school. Through reading, I discovered articles about forensic pathology from my soon to be life-long mentor, Dr. Joseph H. Davis, the former Chief Medical Examiner of Dade County, Florida, which is in Miami. I wrote to Dr. Davis, and although he did not know me, he wrote back. This really impressed me. Basically, he said, "If you really want to do this, read about it." And I did. I read about the science, and I kept reading and I was just enthralled. I volunteered at the local hospitals as a morgue attendant. I volunteered in the laboratory, and I continued to focus my studies on the anatomical development in college. My earliest work was the influence of radiation on eggs.

I had decided to do internal medicine for one year after I finished medical school, knowing that I was going to go into pathology. I went to New York City, and I was, as you guessed, the only black physician on staff at what was considered a community hospital. I wanted a well-rounded education. There was a book out back in the early 1980s called

The House of God, about young physicians in training, and it was very applicable to my situation. Having been at Howard, an inner city hospital, I had learned to do things for myself, and I was very good at procedures. I was one of those people who, when I drew blood, didn't want it to be a painful experience. I wanted to get it right the first time. Because if anyone takes my blood, he or she better get it the first time.

My nickname during my internship was "angle of mercy." The hospital staff always called me when they had a difficult patient. One night, I got called about an elderly lady who I needed to admit to the hospital. It was the middle of the night, and I was really not in the mood, not feeling real pleasant; I was really exhausted. The patient was this little, old, white lady with bare skin and bones. She was so terrified. I looked at her, and I knew she had never seen a black physician in her life.

"Are you the doctor?" she said, frightened.

"Yes."

"Are you going to hurt me?"

"No ma'am," I assured her.

"Everyone keeps sticking me and it hurts," she said.

"I'm going to put an IV in, and I'm not going to hurt you."

She needed chemotherapy, and I kept thinking that I would want someone to treat my grandmother with dignity and respect if she were admitted to the hospital. So I did. I started a butterfly catheter, which is a very tiny intravascular line. Then I admitted her and left her with the nursing coordinator on her floor. I never really thought about it after that; I had basically done my job.

About a month later, I was on the floor working when the head of the medicine department came up to me and said, "I need to see you in my office." I wondered what I had done now. That little, old, white lady had received her chemotherapy and had perked up. She had remembered my act of kindness, putting in the IV without hurting her. She was in bad condition with what I believe was leukemia. This lady was so grateful for the way I treated her that she had knitted me a beautiful multicolored hat and muffler. She also brought me a bouquet of roses, and she said to me, "You're a credit to your race." It was a very emotional moment. That's a phrase I did not want to hear someone say, but I knew in my heart that she meant it innocently. This lady, I think, would look at other black people differently from that point on. While I don't encourage anyone to say it, I know that my grandmother would probably have said the same thing about a white doctor, and I was glad that I was able to make a difference in this lady's opinion.

At Howard University, I learned to treat patients as I would want my loved ones to be treated. The medical students I teach must respect the patient. One of my pet peeves is to observe a young, wet-behind-the-ears medical student walking into a patient's room and saying "How are you doing, Mary?" to a mature senior. I believe, as I was taught as a little girl, that we have to respect our elders, particularly when dealing with another ethnic group. It's very callous to go into a patient's room and assume that person should be on a first name basis. Learning good bedside manner should help medical students understand this concept. To be ill and feel disrespected at the same time is not good for patients.

In my office, everybody has a title. It might be doctor, or it could be Mr. or Mrs. I don't believe in that kind of flip attitude. Some people think it encourages a familiarity, but that's not the point. I think respect. The doctors certainly don't want the support staff calling them by their first names. To me, it's just that everybody has a title and that's because everybody has a role to play. It is one of my beliefs that if everybody were treated as if they were important, if they played a role in a person's health or in the determination of a person's death, we would produce or yield a better product. A very old physician once told me, "The man who cleans the trash doesn't have an education. He doesn't have a title. He doesn't have a lot of money, but he's important because if he doesn't clean the trash, I can't work. So he's due all the respect." I have always taken that to heart. I adhere to some of the golden rules that have helped me to be so successful and have furthered my career, and I get good results from people who I am managing or when I am coordinating their activities. I make them feel that they are part of the team. I remember doctors walking down a hallway, entering a room, or being served at a medical meeting, and not even glancing at the server. I'm not like that. Colleagues would ask, "How come, Dr. Carter, your coats are always here on time?" I never forget the people who are doing the other work because they make my job easy.

During that same internship in New York City where most of the support staff was black, I always made sure I let them know I saw them, and I would say, "Good morning, how are you?" When holidays came around, they brought me some food, some good down home cooking, and they always took care of me just because I gave them back a little bit of dignity!

No one is born a professional. I wasn't born Dr. Carter, I was born Joye Carter. Who knew? I'm not "better than, I'm "different." We need to take that principle to heart. We need to let people know as they are coming up and going through training that they should never forget who they are. It can be taken away in an instant.

While at Wittenberg, after securing a spot in medical school, I attended a job fair with one of my classmates. Now, I had secured a position in medical school with no idea of how I was going to pay for it. I certainly couldn't ask my parents for any more money since they had financed my college education. One of the booths at the job fair was run by the United States Air Force. Wittenberg University, which is in Springfield, Ohio, was very close to Wright Patterson Air Force Base. I have never been a person really big on the military. I was never "cops and robbers" or that kind of thing. But they had an offer that was really a win-win situation. They had the health professions scholarship system: if I committed a certain amount of time after my medical training, they would pay my way through school. *I thought, how bad can this be?* So I signed up, and I got a scholarship. I got a scholarship, a full scholarship, to medical school and, in exchange, I became a commissioned Air Force Officer. My job now was to go to school, make good grades, accrue time and experience. And I did. And that's how I got through medical school with a sigh of relief, and through the summers between years in medical school, I worked in the department of pathology, primarily at the air force base outside of Washington, DC. It was just fascinating. As difficult as medical school was, I was a military officer, and I was able to get involved with death investigation cases that most medical students did not. So it was a really rewarding experience for me.

Getting to medical school is another chapter in itself, but suffice to say, I was successful. I was energized, and I was totally focused on the career.

One experience that I will never forget was the Jones Town Massacre with Jim Jones and the United States citizens that he took with him to form his new land and who essentially committed mass suicide. Those bodies were brought back to Dover Air Force Base. As a medical student, I was involved in the identification process, and it was an experience that is hard to describe. I was there because of that military scholarship.

As an aside, a lot of people frowned on me for being a military officer, but it was a great opportunity, and I encourage young people now to not let dreams be deterred by a lack of money. Seek the money. It's there. I figured my father had given part of his stomach in the Korean War, and all of the tax dollars that he and my mother had paid in cumulatively was a fair exchange for the military to pay for my medical education. I took advantage of that opportunity.

From medical school, I did my postgraduate training, emphasizing on internal medicine and pathology. I ended up meeting Dr. Joe Davis and letting him adopt me as one of his students while in medical school. That relationship continued and strengthened and remains in effect today. After completing all of my pathology residency, I went to Miami to work with Dr. Joe Davis. It was such an honor finally to get to the point I had dreamed of. He knew of my desires, of course. He had known for many years, and he took extra time with me. He allowed me to see the administrative side of being a medical examiner, as well as exposing me to the routine problems of running such an office. Words cannot sum up the experience that he shared with me. I'm so appreciative of that.

Because I was a military officer, I was accruing credit the whole time I was in medical school, postgraduate training, and my forensic pathology fellowship training. When I finished that fellowship period, I joined the United States Air Force active corp. as a chief physician and concurrently as a Major. I went on active duty and became a medical examiner for the United States Air Force. I was headquartered in Washington, DC, with a tri-service unit. I was a federal military forensic pathologist and I worked for the Armed Forces Medical Examiner System. I did this for two and a half years.

Interestingly enough, I had achieved my goal. I studied very hard and passed all of the required board certification, and I started doing something that I thought I would never do. Guess what that was? My mother was a teacher and I always said, "Mother, I will never be a teacher. Teachers are never appreciated. I would never want to do that." But that's just what I did. I taught forensic pathology, and I enjoyed it! I loved knowing that I had made a connection when students said, "I know what you mean." I continued to learn. I traveled around the world as a military officer, to places like Asia, England, South America. Because I loved what I was doing and did it well, I was continuously promoted during my tenure at the

Armed Forces Institute of Pathology. After my fellowship expired, I became an associate medical examiner, then passed my boards, becoming an assistant medical examiner. They appreciated my teaching so I became a deputy chief medical examiner within a year.

During that time period, I was in Washington, D.C., and they were searching for a chief medical examiner. At that time, Washington, D.C. was pretty much in dire straits, and nobody really wanted the chief medical examiner position there. The permanent position had been vacant for ten years; an acting person held the job for those ten years. My first reaction was, "Oh no, I wouldn't even want to consider that." But, stage right, Dr. Davis, with all of his wisdom, sent my name in to be considered and while I was appreciative, I was also very stubborn. No way did I want that hassle. No way did I feel able to do that. But Dr. Davis called me and told me how he became the chief medical examiner of Miami, Florida, when he was in his early thirties, that it was kind of thrust upon him. Dr. Davis said, "You can do it. You have the desire and you're well trained." I thought, *no, I can't do this job nor do I want to.* But he encouraged me.

Because I had gone to medical school in Washington
D.C., I knew a lot of people. So they interviewed me. I thought
about it and decided to go ahead and throw my hat in the ring.
At that time, Washington, D.C., had its first female mayor,
Sharon Pratt-Kelly. I had six months to go in the military and
though there had not been a chief medical examiner in
Washington, D.C., for ten years, all of a sudden, they were
rushing it. I had not finished my three-year commitment to the
Air Force. I actually had only six months to go. Washington,
D.C., was getting a lot of pressure for not having a chief
medical examiner, especially with the escalating murder rate. I
was well trained, I was respected for my knowledge and
professionalism, and I knew Washington. I was in the right
place at the right time. So the process began.

I interviewed with the Washington government
personnel, and something very interesting happened during that
interview process. I got a call one day while I was still in the
Air Force and in the beginning of the interview process. I knew
their needs in Washington. They needed a physician who had
vision, growth, and energy. This call, believe it or not, was
from a man who said, "What is your skin color?" I was taken
aback, "What is your skin color?" he asked.

I said, "I'm brown, why?"

He said "Well, just wanted to know." The caller made it very clear that the government of the District of Columbia was concerned about my skin color.

Now, mind you, I had my hackles up and I said "Look, I'm brown, been brown all my life, hope to God to stay brown until the day I leave this earth, and I happen to realize that I am the only brown person qualified and certified to take this position. If you have a problem with that, you can keep on looking." I was disappointed by this question. And, months later, when I met him, I reminded him of that call saying, "I took this job so that you would understand that qualified people of any color can do this." The sad thing is, he was a person of color who had asked me that very ignorant question. So, you know, you've always got to teach, because ignorance can be cured.

How did I manage to become the chief medical examiner of Washington, D.C., while serving as an Air Force Major? Trust me, it wasn't easy. Because the need was so great in Washington, D.C., and because it was the nation's capital and the homicide rate was so high, Washington, D.C., officials went to the Pentagon to ask for assistance. The

Pentagon plucked me out of the Air Force, put a big bow around my neck, kicked me out, and sent me to Washington, D.C. Now, that wasn't physically agonizing. I met with the Assistant Surgeon General representing Washington, D.C., and I agreed to go to Washington, D.C. I agreed to resign my commission in the Air Force so that I could give my attention twenty-four hours a day, seven days a week to Washington, D.C. I had really wanted to wait six additional months in order to complete my military obligation, but Washington, D.C., needed me. So the Air Force, in its wisdom, rewrote my commission, taking off six months and also retracting two months of paid vacation leave that I had accrued. I resigned my commission, departing the United States Air Force on January 13, 1992. I became the youngest and first black female chief medical examiner for the District of Columbia on January 14, 1992. It was a very short vacation! That's how the saga began. Details of that time in Washington, D.C., will be another chapter. After four and a half years there, I decided that I needed to move on. I applied for the position in Houston, Texas, through a national search, and *voila*! here's where I landed.

What is a Medical Examiner?

I'm often asked, "What is a medical examiner?" I always want to answer by discussing what a medical examiner is not.

A medical examiner is a medical doctor who has specialized in pathology. Pathology is the study of disease. A medical examiner has further specialized, or sub-specialized, in the category of forensic medicine. Forensic medicine is studying diseases and injuries that result in death. In a word, we are the specialists in death. The medical examiner assists law enforcement and the criminal justice system in investigating deaths; therefore, he or she participates on both medical and legal levels. A medical examiner is supposed to be a neutral, fact-finding, observant person. That is sometimes hard for people to understand. The medical examiner's role is to bridge the gap between families and law enforcement. The medical examiner is, by nature, neutral and independent. For me, forsensic medicine, which is what I call my profession, is one of the most noble medical professions there is. I see myself as the one neutral party in the courtroom. I span many different professions and serve as the one link between the family and the entire criminal justice system.

The specialty of forensic medicine is not as well known as others, and unfortunately, we are often characterized as doing what "Quincy" did. I must tell you, I hate it when people say, "Oh, you're 'Quincy', aren't you?" As a matter of fact, it is kind of frightening when I enter a courtroom and I look at the jury and the judge. Sometimes I think, *now which one of these people thinks I should be like 'Quincy'?* I always say, "Quincy did a wonderful thing for our profession. He brought it to television." People began to get an idea of what we do but they also got the wrong idea. The character of Quincy was played by an actor, and the Quincy character was based loosely on the coroner of Los Angeles County. Well, I am a medical examiner, not a coroner. Both medical examiners and coroners investigate death but under different political structures. What's the difference? A coroner is an elected official. A medical examiner is appointed or hired by the governing body of the city or county for whom he or she works. A coroner does not usually have to be a physician, nor does he even have to be a certified forensic pathologist. A coroner has a constituency; that is, the people who elected him may put pressure on him to make certain decisions. And, overall, there are fewer coroner systems in the United States than there are medical examiner systems.

Now for historical prospective, the coroner system is older and was brought over when the first boat landed from England. It was a way of determining who had died, initially for taxation purposes. As we became more sophisticated, or at least as some think in this country, we developed the medical examiner system, consisting of individuals who would not be burdened by political pressure and who would learn a great deal about how the human body functions in order to help all parties understand how and why death occurs.

Quincy usually had only one case a week. Hah! Boy, is that a laugh! Quincy would get extremely emotionally and physically involved with the citizens of his domain. You would see him having dinner, getting into fights, cursing, going out to someone's home, and refusing to go to court. Oh, no. That is not reality.

Quincy also had only one technician who worked around the clock! His assistant, Sam, knew every specialty area in laboratory science. Everything! This man had no life. He obviously put in a lot of overtime, and he worked hand-in-hand with Quincy. He would do things that had not been certified by any other scientific body. That definitely is not reality. In some ways, it's harmful because today's society is so influenced by what they see on TV and at the movies; society needs to be *untrained* to get back to the reality of what medical examiners actually do. Now if I only did one case a week, I'd be out of a job, even though I would get a lot more rest. Certainly, it's not possible, or professional, for the medical examiner to get involved personally with cases, and I certainly would not refuse to go to court. I must admit though, the excitement of Quincy takes away from what we can do. I cannot tell the exact time of death unless I did the crime, and I cannot take one bone and make an entire persona and personality out of it. I wish I could do that, but I do what I can. Remember, a medical examiner is a physician who practices medicine in the medical-legal area, and medicine is not an exact science.

The medical examiner is a trustworthy person. The medical examiner is confident, well spoken, and open to many ideas and many different people. This leads me to the next most frequently asked question. Young people often write to me asking "I want to take an M.E. degree. What do I do?"

I always try to emphasize that they must be a physician to be a medical examiner. They must be willing to set their life for, I would say, at least fourteen years after high school, if that is what they really want to do because pathology is the basis of all medicine. It is the study of disease. It is the study of anatomy. Before I can say how a person died, I have to know how life begins as we know it, how the body functions, and what goes wrong. It is something that is not for everybody. A medical examiner confronts life and death daily. This makes me contemplate my own death and reminds me that for everything I see and do, I have to accept that death is imminent in all of us and that life is short. Again, being a medical examiner is not for everybody, but death is a responsibility that we have to accept in preparing ourselves to do this job.

I would like to stress that there are many related fields in the world of forensic science. Individuals who are forensic scientists work in areas such as forged documents, fingerprint detection, toxicology or testing for drugs in one's system. We have people who work with plant life. They are called forensic botanists. We have forensic engineers. We have forensic photographers. There is a whole world of associated fields, and I would advise you to go to your library, to call your local law enforcement, to perhaps write or check with the FBI. Certainly, get on the Internet. There are several web pages, and there are a couple of main associations that you would want to be familiar with. One organization is The American Academy of Forensic Science, called AAFF, and it is located in Colorado. I am a member of this organization, and we do welcome the opportunity to educate young people about everything we do because we who do it think it is really exciting.

There is another organization called The National Association of Medical Examiners. This is pretty much confined to those who are medical examiners, coroners, and forensic investigators, people who investigate cases for medical examiner offices. This group is headquartered in St. Louis, Missouri, and they also have a website. I invite you contact them, and I wish you luck in doing so.

As a medical examiner, actually as a chief medical examiner, I am a busy person. I play a pivotal role in many things. What does it take to get to be the chief? First, there is sacrifice involved. As the chief, I'm the head person responsible for death investigation. In other words, "the buck stops with me." Currently, I work in Houston, Texas, or Harris County, Texas, which is the fourth largest county in the United

States. I run an office of approximately ninety-five employees. We have a crime lab, and we investigate death under a public law for public cause. We investigate deaths that have occurred violently. These include homicides, motor vehicle accidents, suicides, drug overdoses, and deaths that occur in police custody or government run facilities.

We also investigate deaths of people who have died in public spaces, people who collapse on worksites, and people who have died from injuries or diseases that may pose a public threat, such as someone who dies from food poisoning caused by contaminated food products. We also get involved when there has been an accidental death at a hospital. We may be asked to become involved when there are allegations of unprofessional treatment in hospitals. We must also assume responsibility for mass disaster victims. We are involved in many types of cases.

As the chief medical examiner, my responsibilities vary from minute-to-minute and day-to-day. I call it "putting out fires." It takes a certain amount of flexibility, a certain strength of character, and knowledge and patience, above all. I have to accept responsibility for the good and the bad things that occur in my jurisdiction. That means I have to realize that everything is not always going to go my way. I remind myself that I do not go to work to make friends. I tell my staff, "You're not here to be a friend. You're here to do your job, to do your best for the community."

This means that I must like myself because I can't avoid being human, and sometimes I can't avoid errors. What I can do is to practice humility and patience. When something happens that I don't like or is unfortunate, I have to step back, take a deep breath, count to ten (or longer), and deal with the situation. I must remember that every situation can be unique. I can never forget that when I deal with death on a daily basis and with grieving families, these people are trusting me to do the right thing. People who are grieving are not in their usual emotional state of mind and may say or do a variety of abnormal things. I am aware of this fact and have grown accustomed to it.

Yes, I've been called derogatory names. I've been threatened with bodily harm. I've been cursed at and spat on. I've had people in obvious shock carry on a conversation yet have no idea what they are talking about. Knowing how to deal with these situations comes with training and experience.

How Did You Become Chief Medical Examiner?

This is another question that is frequently asked of me, but it is certainly not a one-answer question.

I became the chief medical examiner in Houston, Texas, after a national search. I had been the chief medical examiner in Washington, D.C. How did I become the chief medical examiner in Washington, D.C?

Let's start from the very beginning. I was introduced to the field of pathology as a high school student. My family had relocated from our small town in Ohio to the larger city of Indianapolis, Indiana. I attended Shortridge High School, and after expressing an interest in the healthcare profession, I worked at a local hospital during the summer between my freshman and sophomore years. Eli Lilly Pharmaceutical Company, headquartered in Indianapolis, provided me with the job. So at fourteen, I got a job in the kitchen, assisting in cooking.

My mother would certainly say that I was never really the best cook at that age. I was actually probably more of a danger because I was left-handed, and I always cut toward my body. Anyway, I was helping prepare breakfast for the patients in the kitchen, which was in the basement of the hospital. And guess what else was there: the morgue.

I had burned my hand making coffee, and the staff basically told me to get out of there and do something else because they felt I couldn't do anything there. I left the kitchen area and happened to observe the bodies being wheeled into the morgue. I got REALLY curious, so I peeked through the window. I saw that they were examining the bodies, filling out identifying paperwork, storing the bodies, and then releasing the bodies to funeral homes. I became interested in what I was seeing, and I got a little peek at an autopsy and of the pathologist examining the body, and I must tell you, I was extremely curious. I was not grossed out, and I wanted to know more.

Trust me, when I went home and told my mother what I had seen, she was not ecstatic. Nonetheless, I was curious, and I began to read about pathology and forensic pathology through the library. My curiosity continued to peak, and, as I studied anatomy in biology in school, I knew what I wanted to do. I was bitten early, and nothing detracted from that. I was just curious and more interested, and I set my sights on becoming a medical examiner. At that point in my development, it was really not an issue of my gender or my color. That didn't stop me. I never really thought about it. I loved the profession and read all types of books on the subject.

As a young girl, I realized that not everyone was interested in dead bodies. But I kind of let myself go into that futuristic dream world and saw that I was interested and that I could do this. I knew that I was going to do this. I observed how our family physicians treated patients and I visited their clinics. I thought to myself, *no, I can't do that; it's just not the same thing.* I knew early on as a high school student that I was very health conscious, always. It was natural for me. I wasn't real big on taking medications. I didn't like to take aspirin when I had a headache; I liked to rest.

I was curious about what happened to animals. Remember: I was living in Indiana. A big highway runs through Indianapolis, Interstate 70. Driving there, I saw corn, or dead animals. Often I saw both, but it was the dead animals that caught my eye. What happened? What was that stiff bloating stage? Most people will say, "Oh, how gross." My mother's response was, "Oh, yuck!" But my mother and I were different people. I was an animal lover. I had a deep curiosity about animal life and insect life. My mother was very squeamish and I was not. I remember telling her "Mom, when I grow up, I'm going to have a big house with a pool because I want to have an Anaconda and room for my dogs."

My mother wondered where her youngest child had come from. I loved animals. I was also fascinated by reptiles. Even to this day, I still like to go to the zoo. All this seemed very natural to me, and I was able to get jobs because of what I liked to do - - growing plants, feeding the animals. Lucy the Ladybug was one of my pets. She lived with me and on me for several weeks, then just disappeared.

Because of my curiosity and interest in animals, I was able to propel myself and to excel in the earth sciences in high school, and in college, I worked as a laboratory assistant, taking care of the fruit flies. I grew them for DNA and helped isolate DNA material for research study at Wittenberg University. Because of my interest and my good grades in the physical sciences, I got another job at the courtesy of Eli Lilly at Indiana University. During the summer, I worked in the Department of Pathology at the University Medical School. Now I was a college student with no degree, but I had the energy and the interest, or the fearlessness I should say, so I was employed to take care of rats. Oh, yeah, I was truly a "gopher" (go for). I fed them, cleaned their cages, and I realized how many rats lived in the walls of that medical school. I was able to get into the Department of Neuropathology and to assist the pathologists. Basically what I did was help make the diamond-edged knife blades used to cut the thin microscopic sections. I also took care of cats. Yes, at that time, laboratories were using animals for research, so I cared for some of the cats too.

During that summer between my sophomore and junior years in college, I witnessed a completed autopsy, a forensic autopsy. I had actually gone to the morgue with one of the doctors. I tagged along after begging and pleading, and I remember the doctor saying very sternly, "Don't touch anything; it's a dirty, dirty place. If you drop a pen, leave it." Well, I thought, *how bad can this be?* I entered the autopsy suite behind the doctor, and I just listened. There was a pathologist examining the body of a young man who had died following a motorcycle accident. There was a police officer observing the autopsy, and the doctor told the police officer that the victim was not wearing a helmet. He estimated the speed of the motorcycle. He demonstrated for the police officer and for me the marks on the decedent's legs that showed pedal marks.

He explained that the decedent had lost control and had died from head injuries. The reason I was in that place was because the family of the decedent had donated his brain to research, and since I was working in neuropathology, they were going to be able to do some studies. I was just in my element then. I was not afraid. I was so excited that I could learn so much through examinations without talking to a patient. Boy, that was it for me! I knew what I was going to do, and I would never be persuaded to do anything else.

How Does It Feel To Be The First
Black Female Chief Medical Examiner?

I hear this question when giving talks to students and when making public presentations. That's a very strange question for me, and I always start off by saying, "I have no other frame of reference to answer by. I was born black and female and, God willing, I will die black and female." The question is strange because I know that I am a rarity, but at the same time, I can't say how it feels to be anything else. I'm not green; I'm not white; I'm not male. I think people are always surprised to find out that I don't fit the mold of media portrayals of medical examiners. Some people mistake my voice – on the phone or the radio – as that of another ethnic group, and I have this to say to them, "You shouldn't make assumptions."

People ask, "Where are you from?"

"I'm from the Midwest." I reply. "I have a flat, non-accent tone, and that's the way everybody talks where I come from."

Some people try to frame the question a little differently. They find out who I am, and then they say to me, with a look of disbelief on their face, "You're so Wh….." This is followed by a prolonged silence. "You're so wh..., young, yeah, that's it, young, you're so young."

When I look the person in the eye, I know he/she wanted to ask something else like, "You are female, do not sound black, look too young to be certified and experienced – how did you get this job?"

I suppose most people ask me because they want to understand the pressures of being the first one. Many people are aware of the awkward position I am in and are genuinely concerned about my stress level. Overall, the problems I encounter are only unique to others who have been the first to do something different. The next black woman, hopefully, will not have to face this kind of question in the field of forensic medicine.

I started off talking about the question I receive so often: "What's it like to be the chief medical examiner?" I kind of got away from the topic because so many things come to mind. As the chief medical examiner, I am in charge of the entire operation, a very big, frightening responsibility. Sometimes my words, or how I use or phrase them, can mean the difference between a long sentence, a life sentence, or even the death penalty. I accept the responsibility that goes along with the title; however, sometimes people will view me as a black woman before they view me as a highly trained, skilled professional person. I work with death, a topic people never really want to address. As the chief medical examiner, I am responsible for the good and bad that happens to my office on a daily basis, whether I am present or not. (I could be in the midst of an important situation when the pager goes off, such as being at a wedding, in church, or even on a date, but again, that is part of being a responsible person.)

When I first began the position in Houston, I read a message to all of the section leaders in my department, and I stated that I was a strong woman who takes responsibility for her actions and always moves toward her goals. I wanted my staff to understand that I would accept the responsibility for the office, good and bad. I would fulfill a nurturing role, but I would also hold them accountable for their actions so that we might all work together to solve the problems and answer the questions that are posed to us. This type of responsibility puts additional stress on my life, requiring support from outside sources and a strong inner foundation. I think that is what equips me to handle this lifestyle.

At some point, people need to take the "black" out of it and the "female" and just leave the person who performs the job and who is the best trained. That's how I try to answer that question. I don't have any other perspective. If I did, people probably wouldn't be asking that question. I know that they seldom ask a white male that question because he is the norm. When someone becomes leader or first, she must overcome additional battles; I accept that. I know that, at times, my career is difficult because I am the first, but I sure hope I'm not the last. The best way I can secure this prediction is to mentor others and make sure that other people follow my lead. Once I begin to do my work, the people who ask what it's like will see that it doesn't matter about the gender or the color of the examiner. What matters is, who is the best *person* for the position.

For a long time, I have believed in the old adage, "each one, teach one," and I try to stress that it is very important to help others aspire to reach goals similar to my own. It appears that many times professionals get to a certain level, and, all of a sudden, they don't want anyone else to get there. Trust me, I have too much work and too many requests for my abilities to represent minority issues. There are so many things that happen to minorities that involve police deaths, unanswered questions about death, and mistrust of the white medical community. I get calls regarding these issues from all over the country. I am excited about someone else becoming the next black chief medical examiner so that we can continue to show that I'm not just one; I'm not just the exception; I didn't just get through. They didn't lower the rails for me; I didn't leap over the hurdle; I went through fire like everybody else.

Another story comes to mind. I was taking my pathology board certification examination with another colleague of mine, who happened to be a black female; we had really prepared ourselves for this ordeal. We had studied day and night for a year, she, in Los Angeles, and me, in Miami. We decided to room together while we took our examinations, and we had a little scream therapy going on. We were tired and nervous because of the difficult exam, but we were determined to give it our best. We were well trained and determined to do the one-pass special. We had taken the first part of the three-day long examination and were in the elevator going back to our hotel room. A white male was on the elevator, along with several of his colleagues, and he said very loudly, "Well, it's a known fact that forty percent of white males who take this test pass on the first run, and, you know, the other ones don't do as well." We were, of course, still in the back of the elevator, and we both took out our sunglasses and put them on to cover our bloodshot eyes. As we got out of the elevator on our floor, we turned around and said, "Until now!" and snapped our fingers. We went back to our room and vigorously practiced our scream therapy. That man obviously overlooked the fact that my friend and I had determination and training and we were earning that same degree of certification as he and his colleagues. He thought that just because he was white, he would pass. This is terribly presumptuous.

I was more determined after that incident to go back and make sure I had the right answers, to let my brain lead me where no man had gone before. As luck and prayer would have it, when we received our envelopes, YES, we had both passed! We both knew. We had shown that guy that he shouldn't have counted us out! That was also important because I felt that examination was typical of standardized tests given in the United States today. As I read over many of those test questions, I was relieved and grateful to my mother for hammering in all those nuances of grammar in the English language. I noted that just recognizing an article or an adverb or adjective would change the entire meaning of the question. I realized that these nuances took minorities and foreign physicians out of the running. I always tell students to make sure they review their grammar because the questions are tricky. Ever so slightly, a "the" versus an "a" may completely alter the question's answer. A good example is when I tell someone I determine "a" cause of death, which means a "general" cause of death. When I say, we have determined "the" cause of death, that's the cause of death that applies to a particular person. That's very important; I can't over-emphasize enough the power of education.

So how does it feel to be the first black female chief medical examiner? To sum it up, it feels great, because I know, I won't be the last.

What Was Your Worst Case?

Usually the person asking me this question is one who has just said, "I could never do what you do. I would be terrified."

It appears that people ask me this question for two reasons: 1) they are very curious as to why I do what I do, and 2) some of them want to live vicariously through hearing stories about what I do. This question comes up at the most inappropriate moments, usually at a social situation or right at the time of a sit-down dinner when the entree is about to be served. Generally, I give the same answer: "I don't have a worst case, and I don't carry a set of cases around in my mind to talk about." In all honesty, I have to answer, "The worst case is the next case." I just don't believe in categorizing cases. I have always felt that the case I am involved with now is the most important to a particular family. It is very difficult to take just one and say this is the worst case of all because I never know what's coming next. I could discuss cases that have been the most sensitive or that have more of an effect, particularly on my staff, and these are usually cases involving deaths of innocent people, especially children or victims of terrorists or drunk drivers. Cases where the decedent was completely innocent in their actions affect the staff. It's terribly heart wrenching to view the remains of a child who has been battered to death. It is particularly hard on those in law enforcement to get involved in investigating the deaths of children. Yet, and still, for everybody who has lost a loved one, there is a worst case, the ones who are surviving this unexpected ordeal and finding a way to go on.

As medical examiners we place importance on everybody. Death equates people. We cannot evade death. If we are rich, if we are from a certain ethnic background, young, old, rich or poor, famous, infamous, or homeless, it doesn't matter. There is no escaping it. I am compassionate to each individual I examine who has died.

My grandfather died around the same time that President John F. Kennedy was assassinated, and I recall all of the media attention that was given to the President's death. Certainly for us, as a country, that event will forever remain one of the most important historical incidents. But my mother observed that although my grandfather was not the most important man in the world, to her he was the most important individual. I try to carry that with me into every case. I don't want people to feel that they are going to be treated differently in death than any other person. We do that too much in health care. We do that too much in the media. Certainly, the media portrays the deaths of the rich and famous as unfortunate tragedies, turning each one into an event. The media frenzy that surrounded the death of Princess Diana was an example that maybe we have gone too far. I think sometimes the media sends a message about death that causes an unrealistic view that the rich and famous shouldn't die, or that all rich and famous people should live to be a ripe old age. Granted, the death of Princess Di and her fiancée was a tragedy. How many other people died that day in Paris, France, who received absolutely no recognition? Were their lives really less important to their loved ones?

Another example was the most recent tragedy of John Kennedy, Jr. Extremely tragic! I listened and watched all the media around this airplane accident, and my very first thought was certainly of the poor Kennedy family, that they had to grieve so publicly and so often. Yes, it was a tragic loss. My second thought was of the family of the two women who also died in that plane crash and who were almost dealt with as afterthoughts. I really think that is a fault of our media. No one can ever explain the loss one goes through when that person is taken from one's life suddenly. And so, it's important to stress that there are no favorites in my mind. There is no one worst case scenario. I think my time in the military taught me more about the waste of young lives, those individuals fighting for their country who became embroiled in conflict either through weaponry or hand-to-hand combat because some other people in a faraway land decided to have a war. After hundreds of bodies came my way, I developed a theory. It's not a new theory. It's something that has been talked about over the ages, but I believe that if the individuals who decided to go to war actually thought about it, that war would probably be over very quickly; it would probably be a lot less painful, and certainly, there would be few fatalities.

In the military, the phrase "For God and Country" is important. Family came a whopping third. The killing of other people, especially innocent people, disturbed me. When I examined the remains of people who died in war, I imagined what their families felt, what kind of loss. For many, to lose a son or daughter in battle is to gain a hero, but they also lose that loved one forever. Is that a worst case for me? No, but it is probably a worst case for those individuals' families.

Certainly, when we read about deaths that occur in an airplane accident, we selfishly focus on the crash of a plane, but not on the individuals who died in that aircraft. But the loss of these people is significant to the families who suffered that personal loss.

Remember the man who flew into the White House, committing suicide? The media suggested that the tragedy was that someone was trying to harm the President, yet a family lost a loved one. Again, when someone dies tragically and unexpectedly, suddenly, or for a senseless reason, it is very painful, when I get involved with violence, I must recognize that there are going to be many victims. The dead are victims who no longer feel pain. But the survivors, the loved ones, the family of the dead, as well as the family of the perpetrators must go on and live with the tragedy. Many times I discuss findings in homicide cases with families who have lost a loved one to violence. Their pain and suffering goes on for many years, much longer than the brief media exposure that they receive. Everyone has his or her own time for grieving and, to those people, the loss of their loved one is probably one of the most important events in their lives.

The media, I believe, plays a very distinct role in the violence that occurs, particularly in the black community. When I was the Chief Medical Examiner in Washington, D.C., I was appalled because we observed, year in and year out, the number of homicides, black on black crime, in particular young black men, dying over the most senseless acts of violence, like looking at someone funny, envying an article of clothing, or stepping on someone's foot at a party. What a tragedy! Most of these types of homicides, if covered in the media at all, were on a back page, a little column of sheer numbers with no faces or names. Yet, at the beginning of every year, there was intense coverage when the first white person was killed in Washington, D.C. I developed a slogan: "Back Page, Just Us." So when I'm asked the question, "what is the worst case," it is always relative. It's a relative issue.

When people ask, "what's your worst case?" they are also trying to understand why I do death investigations. They don't want to see what I do or how I do it. They're a little squeamish, or they find it distasteful, but they want to understand <u>why</u> I do it, which is difficult to explain. Some people want to live vicariously; they don't want to see a human body examined or completely opened and the organs dissected, yet they want to hear the story because it's more entertaining when they are disassociated. I oftentimes just can't imagine my acquaintances really wanting to use my stories for dinnertime entertainment, but it happens frequently. I say to my acquaintances, "My really good friends who have known me forever and who know me as Joye, wouldn't do that. They realize when I'm out in public, which is rare, that I need a little downtime like everybody else." So I simply say: "This is not good dinner table conversation."

For me, the worst case is relative to the situation and the people affected most by the loss of a loved one. I am grateful that I have retained the ability to treat everyone in need of comfort with the same level of compassion and respect. I feel this is one of my most special God-given talents.

Why Do You Wear Your Hair Like That?

It is difficult to believe that this question about hair comes up during a professional scientific talk, but it does, rather frequently. I have come to terms with my hair, my lifestyle, and what works for me as an individual. I have chosen to wear my hair natural and not to color my premature gray, which I love. I have avoided discussing physical beauty because how I feel about myself on the inside is not always how other people see me. We need to rely on ourselves, not others' perceptions of us. I also had to contend with a traditional standard of beauty at a very early age. I grew up in an environment surrounded by white children who looked completely different from me. Later, it was the beautiful women of color who graced the covers of the new ethnic magazines. That was it! Where did I fall? I was very young when the black consciousness of the sixties occurred, but it affected me. It touched me in a very profound and personal way because I remember seeing pictures of black women with brown skin, kinky hair, wide noses, and bigger than size five bodies standing up and saying, "I am a black American and I deserve equal treatment."

In the black community, on Saturdays, particularly in the sixties, little girls would sit patiently while their hair was done. It was usually combed with a hot comb to straighten it so it would look good for church the next day. We would all troop in, me and my three sisters, and get our hair done one by one. But I would wake up on Sunday morning and my hair would be frizzy. My mother tried everything. My other sisters looked like they had just had their hair done, and mine looked like it had not ever been done. That was a source of frustration for me, early on. There I was, sticking out like a sore thumb, again. This strange head of hair just wanted to do its own thing. I hated the shear torture and cringing from that heat on the nape of my neck. When the movement came around in the late sixties, I was reading about the activity in Watts. I had already suffered the effects of a chemical relaxer as a child, probably in the fourth or fifth grade. Because the relaxer ruined my hair, I started wearing it natural. I think I was one of the first children in my neighborhood to do so. It was pure freedom!

Somehow, in this little tiny town, I found a hair pick with a black fist on it, and I loved that pick! I loved the feeling of my natural hair. I must say I was active too. I was not the little girl with ruffles, afraid of snakes and bugs. I was a tomboy. I loved to climb trees. I loved all kinds of animals. I was a runner, and I would try to play football whenever I could. Natural hair fit my lifestyle. I just loved that feeling of being me, and not having to endure that pulling and the heat from the straightening comb.

Interestingly enough, as a social commentary, hair was one of the things that people of color used as weapons against other people of color. We haven't come very far because we're still looking at each other and judging ourselves on the length and texture of our hair, I must say, perhaps moreso, than other ethnic groups judge us.

I continued to wear my hair natural and actually, it was really quite a huge head of hair. We used to say that if you could see our forehead, our Afros weren't big enough. I still have my picture showing me as "Miss Boss Afro, 1974."

My hair set me apart because it was on my head, and I was always just a little out there, sometimes all alone. The adventures I had with my hair were very interesting. I remember, in college, I wore my hair in an Afro, the modified shag shape of the mid- nineteen seventies look, but one particular incident made me so proud. In the seventies a lot of women were starting to get away from natural hair. Hair care companies were developing the no-lye hair relaxers, advertised as being more gentle for black women. I wasn't having that. I was too poor in college to worry about my hair, and I had learned to cut it myself. In fact, I made extra money cutting other people's hair. One day, Gwendolyn Brooks, the former Poet Laureate of Illinois, came to Wittenberg. She read a poem entitled "For Those Women That Still Have Their 'Fros'."

I stood up, just as proud as I could be, as she read this poem, and I was on fire! Yes! This is me! My sense of self had risen to the top, and I just basked in the glory of the "natural kink," and I became more, "Happy to be Nappy!" Brooks was describing *me*. My hair fit my active lifestyle: early classes, dancing, fencing. I would not allow people to define me by my hairstyle.

When I started medical school, at the most famous of the historically black colleges, Howard University, I could count the number of women in my class who were wearing natural hair and have fingers remaining. To me, it was a sad commentary. Black people still judged each other by their personal appearance. Now, with the exception of plastic surgery, we don't have control over what we look like, and our appearance changes over the years. Looks will not last forever.

So, if you base your acceptance simply on what you look like, you will be disappointed since it's not the outside you come to love; it's the inner self, the ear, the listener, the confidant. That's what counts in the end. We sell the physical appearance, though, in our society. In the black community, instead of anointing and celebrating our differences, we were to look down upon one another. It's amazing to find this attitude existing in the seventies, the late nineteen seventies, at a majority black historical college. But it did.

When I joined the Air Force, I was wearing my hair natural and short, but I was busy and my hair grew longer. I braided or cornrowed it. I was always sure it was neat and did not obstruct my view, and I was continuously challenged. I was called into a conference by an officer who said, "You know, you're the only black Air Force officer wearing your hair in these braids and it's against the regulations."

I had to pull out the book of regulations. I said, "My hair is neat and it's above the collar." I was getting it done in a style that was pulled all the way back and formed a bun at the nape of my neck. My hat fit, my helmet fit. What was the problem? I was forced to challenge this.

The response I received was, "It doesn't look right. It doesn't look uniform."

And, again, I had to challenge. "I don't look uniform, but my skills are. If my hair is neat and above my collar, have I broken the law? It's my civil rights at question." I continued to wear my hair in braids after that episode in the military.

When I became the Medical Examiner for the District of Columbia, another funny situation arose. My grandmother asked me to let my hair grow; she wanted to see it long again. And I did. She is probably the only person who could ask me to do something with my hair that I would do. I loved her, and I did it for her. I let my hair grow, and I ended up needing to relax it to control it, and all the while it felt like I was using an illegal substance. Why do I say that? I had this hair that was soft and thick, hard to relax, a very sensitive scalp. Difficult! It also grew fast when I got a relaxer, and I had to get one at least every four weeks. It was like taking drugs. I had to go get a chemical fix. I felt repressed. I felt tied to my hairdresser. I felt enslaved. I resented this chemical relaxer. I didn't feel free. I couldn't dance. I was afraid to exercise. I couldn't go swimming. As you can tell, I loved my grandmother! And one day, my sister Sharon came to visit me, and she was wearing this beautiful short, neat, natural hair. We went out to get our hair done, and I took her to my beauty shop. She went in and got a little trim, she was in and out of that chair in twenty minutes. This was July in Washington, D.C., mind you, way over ninety degrees! It took me two hours for the wash, the set, the curl, and the style. We walked outside after that. My sister looked gorgeous, neat, and cool with the wind blowing through her hair. I got outside, and the humidity hit me like a slap in the face. I looked like Bozo. My hair took on humidity and swelled, and it looked like I had never had anything done to it. I told myself then and there, that I had had it with chemical relaxers.

How did I go from chemical relaxers to natural? It's not any easy transition. So I decided to get my hair braided and let it grow out and then I would get it cut. I wore my hair braided again. I always kept it in a neat style. I have always enjoyed my hair looking neat at all times. At this particular time, I was growing out my hair and had kind of become attached to the braid styles, so I continued to wear them over several months, changing them every two to four weeks. On one occasion, I was in between braids and had to go to some sort of public meeting, a forum. I had brushed my hair, applied a little oil, pulled it back, and put on a hat. I was standing at this affair, and I thought I looked pretty decent when one of my colleagues came up to me and said very cattily, "Oh, you took those braids out. You know, I never liked those things in the first place. I'm glad you came to your senses because, you know, in your position, you ought to be looking better than that." I couldn't believe my ears.

I turned around and looked at her and I said, "Excuse me?" I said, "This is just a temporary change. Tomorrow I'm going to get my hair braided again, and I'm glad to know you never liked it because I never did it for you in the first place, I did it for me, and in my position I do not think that my patients would mind how I wear my hair. And, as far as meeting the public, I appreciate someone coming to me being as natural as they can be. I wouldn't want a white person coming to me wearing an Afro wig. Why should I pretend to be something I'm not?" She looked at me with a gaping mouth and had nothing much else to say. I thought about it for awhile and I said, "You know, however you choose to wear your hair is your business as long as you don't put it in my food, swing it into my face, or use it to clog my drains. Why should anybody care? Now granted, I don't want to see a huge Afro in front of me at the movie theatre nor do I want someone spiking my eye out with these new modern styles some teens are wearing. But is that all the further we have come?"

I don't want to say that natural hair is better than relaxed. For me, natural just works better. For other people, relaxed works better. One of my most favorite singers, James Brown, has always had chemicals in his hair, but I don't see anyone demanding that he turn in his NAACP card. I mean, haven't we come far enough in the new millennium to say it's what your hair is covering that's important? Are we going to be tied to the secondary beauty standards that really have nothing to do with us? When is it going to stop?

Even when I went to South Africa, after they had their first set of elections and I was privileged to travel there, there were things I was saddened to observe. I went out to Cape Town to put on a clinic, and I observed that the women were reading a magazine, *The South African Ebony,* that was filled with ads for chemical relaxers and skin lighteners. I was horrified because many of the people that I was seeing as patients in the clinic were coming in, not with injuries and bites or natural diseases but for chemical burns from applying skin lighteners. Skin bleaching cream! They were coming with hair broken off, coarse and brittle, from incorrect use of hair relaxers. In my mind, it was like viewing what it must have been like in this country when slavery was abandoned. We're supposed to be enlightened; we're supposed to accept ourselves. Someone needed to say that it was okay to have kinky hair, to be different, nappy but happy. We've got to start here to say, and believe, that black is beautiful!

It disturbs me when I see ads in the magazines and on TV with these chemical relaxers that are now developed for little girls. One particular company had a contest for the prettiest little girl. I remembered my own initial thoughts of failure and fear, and for all the other little girls judged by a standard of beauty they cannot attain, that wasn't meant for them, and for all the little girls who are going to grow up with thin patches in the front of their head because of the chemicals being applied too early. When are we going to say, "Hey, celebrate whatever you have? Do the best with what you have. Be happy."

That's not all there is to life – hair! If it wouldn't grow back so fast I might even consider shaving it all off to prove a point. Are you looking at the outside or listening to the inside? What's it all about? To me, it's what its covering. And I ask people, "If this is what you are looking at when I'm giving you a talk, did you hear anything I said?"

One young man approached me recently and said, "I've just got to tell you, your hair is beautiful." He meant my gray. I do not color my gray hair, and there is a very good reason. It's my inheritance. I did not get this from the pressures of my job. It's not from stress. It's a badge of love. I consider it a badge of love because it's a connection. On my mother's side of the family, the women gray prematurely. When I was twenty-four, I developed a gray streak right up the front of my hairline. That gray streak occurred when my father died. Instantly! I looked in the mirror at this beautiful gray streak in the front of my hair, and there was never, ever any doubt about my heredity, my gift from my mother was my hair. I loved it! It also demonstrated the pain that I felt when my father left me as a young medical student. I could never color it. It's part of belonging. And I must admit I was very proud to be the baby, the youngest, but also the most gray. So today, I'm grateful, I'm thankful, and I'm cool with my curls.

I was recently asked what I would leave in the time capsule for the woman's museum in Dallas, Texas? I didn't hesitate to say, "I would leave the straightening comb and the box of no lye cream relaxer and a nice smiling face saying, "I'm happy to be nappy!"

What Are Some of the Highlights
of Your Career?

This is a difficult question to answer because my career
has been so varied. There have been so many aspects to my job
that I just can't pick out a few favorite images, although there
are some that flash more in my memory than others.

As a military officer and federal medical examiner, I
was able to travel to so many places and to meet so many
people that it helped to form some of my adult opinions about
life and the common human plight. Traveling helped me to see
the commonness of situations and the tragedies of war. I left
the military feeling that there is no reason for war to occur, just
no reason. There is no reason for men and women to lose their
lives over oil disputes or the superiority of an ethnic group.

I really enjoyed the opportunities to learn first hand
about different cultures, of people living in South America and
Panama. I made several trips to Panama, surrounding the
Panama invasion and the Noriega conflict, and I felt disgraced
by the condition of Panama and the way the Panamanians lived
and the way they were fenced out of their land, the Panama
Canal. It was embarrassing to me as an American to see what

we had done and allowed to happen. Imagine if in your country, your own country, you could not go to certain parts of town. Is that hard to imagine? Oh, I don't think so. Many people in our country feel restricted from going to many parts of their cities. I know that from working with young people who haven't been able to travel across the city to take advantage of museums or who, to this day, are not able to buy homes in certain parts of cities. What city? Name one. Written or unwritten rules still occur.

I was fortunate to be able to visit South Africa with an international team and to make a presentation before their Supreme Court members. I was so honored. Even after Apartheid had ended, I realized that I was being treated differently because I was an American citizen. By addressing the Supreme Court and the superior judges on neutral death investigations, I hoped to help leave the message that any person, white or black, with the same qualifications, could do the job. It was also eye opening to look at South Africa trying to rebuild and reconstruct, and I have vivid pictures in my mind of what our country went through after slavery was declared illegal.

The media portrays South Africa as war torn with ghettos and shanties. But it's not so different from parts of America such as Washington, D.C., Houston, Chicago, Indianapolis, or Sacramento. These cities all have areas of low income. They all have areas that make you feel ashamed to be a citizen. This is what I found in South Africa, that there really wasn't much difference. Oh, yes, as a country, we complained about Apartheid in South Africa, but did we not have the same thing in America? We don't call it the same, yet we have barriers set up where if we are not careful, if we are not assisted, those barriers will affect us for the rest of our life.

I have had some personal victories. One was taking a stance against presumed consent laws for human tissue transplantation that I felt took advantage of individuals who didn't have knowledge of the law or access to legal representation. I was invited to discuss the issue with Minister Farrakhan at his home. Having had several conversations with him, I learned that he was a very learned and talented man who understood the needs of the transplant community and pledged to support it as long as it was equal and fair. That was quite exciting for me. It brought about an exchange of ideas and, I think, a lifelong respect.

Some of my cases enabled me to meet the needs of celebrities. I don't think it would be responsible of me to name names; they know who they are, and I can only say that having worked with me, I hope they have different opinions of what people of color can do, as well as people of different means.

I'm not one to reflect back constantly on the past, but I can say that all these experiences added together make career highlights. I'm also not one to reflect upon things that I have done as an individual, yet it has been heartwarming to have peer recognition and community recognition. I have been very blessed to have that happen, to have people who support me in my mission to be a public servant. There have been times of stress, particularly in Houston, Texas, where black, brown, and white have come together to support me, all the time realizing that my aim has been to be an honest public servant. That means a lot when sometimes I feel like I am fighting a war all by myself.

In my mind, degrees and personal accomplishments are nice, but in the end I don't think they mean much if I can't address another person with respect or look him or her in the eye, or help someone in need. That has been the benefit to me because in the end we all go the same way, no matter what. I hope people get that message and take it to heart. We are all in this together. We all have a role to play. No one is small or insignificant. All those other trappings can be taken away in a moment's notice. Think about it.

How Did You Develop Such A Strong Sense of Self?

This question is usually posed by young people, both male and female, after I describe the path to my career. I like to go back and explain that we all have a sense of self inside, that we just need to develop it, sometimes through an external force and sometimes through an internal force. For me, I can look back at some stages where I needed a strong sense of self to persevere. I think I stated earlier that as a child I wasn't all that full of self-confidence at times. I can recall a couple of instances where I needed to support myself emotionally.

I previously discussed that I was an avid reader. I started out with mythology and fairy tales. I was struck as a child by the essence of the fairy tales, and I extrapolated a personal message from fairy tales which I call "the mirror on the wall" theory. This is a great teaching tool. In the fairy tale of Snow White, the queen gazing at her reflection asks, "Who's the fairest one of all?" And the mirror would answer back, "Well, it's you, Queen." In reality that's true. The reflection in the mirror is you. The person in the mirror is who you need to do your best for and look your best for. That's you! If you don't think highly of yourself, is anyone else going to? I had to think well of myself. I had to say, "You're OK."

Like any other child, you are a product of your environment. I remember wondering to myself as a very small child why I didn't look more like my mother. To me, my mother was so beautiful. She was the kind of woman who had a beautiful face that didn't need makeup, and I kept hoping that I would grow up to look like her. While I have a few of her characteristics, I didn't come out the spitting image. One of my other sisters did. I always used to say, "Gee, I wish I looked like my mother." One day, though, I decided I looked like me, and there is no one else who looks like me; I'm a little bit of everybody. This came true when I was about to go into the end of middle school, and my hair began to turn red in the summers. Now I was, and still am, what I call a nice, rich, cinnamon brown and it felt a little odd to have my hair changing color. There I was again sticking out like a sore thumb. I decided that it was my hair. My mother and grandmother told me that I had a great-uncle who had red hair, and he was a very dark-skinned black man. I felt like I was belonging a little bit. It made me a little unique, and I embraced it. For several years, I had this strangely colored red and dark brown hair on my head. I decided to like myself because I was given two choices: like or dislike myself. I chose to like myself.

I have adapted my feelings of self-like over the years, and at many times that was the only thing that helped preserve my self-esteem. I base a lot of that on my education, my early experiences of knowing there were so many different people and so many little unique things about them. I guess I can't express that enough. It's so important to let your children know that it's okay for them to be themselves. We have to remember that it takes all kinds to make a world.

A friend of mine once told me a story about why he felt he was included into a group at a time when he stood out. He said, "Look at all the wild flowers. God didn't make a garden just full of daisies. Daisies are among the roses and the tulips, the thorny plants and the green plants, and together it's so spectacular." To me, it's kind of like what we all bring to the table. You know, you can have salt and pepper. You have plain white salt, you have plain black pepper, but doesn't seasoned salt add just the right amount of flavoring. It makes that gumbo so good, and isn't that what gumbo is all about, all those different flavors and textures together? We just have to start teaching kids that it's okay, that different is better.

Different is just as good, and there is nothing wrong with being different.

Many years ago when I was working in Washington, D.C., as the Chief Medical Examiner, I was asked to give a presentation for career day at a high school. This high school was a rather affluent one, and they had a small population of African-American and Hispanic American students. I wanted to make that day special because at that time there was a saying going around and a practice in the Washington area, and many other cities, that studying wasn't cool, being smart wasn't in, and I wanted to let them know that learning *was* cool. I decided to be really different that day. I could have put a dark suit on and been very sober and given my little talk, but I decided to have fun with this. So I put on a vividly purple suit, form-fitting, I must say, just the right length to the mid-knee, and I said, "Let's play some James Brown." When they began to announce me, all the dignitaries were on the dais, the superintendents and the school board members, some very prominent business people, all sitting there looking quite sober, quite serious, and I said, "No, I want to come from the back." I came dancing down the aisle to James Brown, and I could see the shocked looks on my colleague's faces. "The Medical Examiner is dancing down the aisle!" But I didn't really care about their expressions. Every eye of every student was on me. I got to the stage and said, "I want you all to know: you don't have to give up your soul to be a professional. I want you all to know that this dancing got me through medical school. I want you all to know that when I have a bad day, if you come around my house, you will hear some loud music, and you might see me flipping across the room or screaming at the top of my lungs, but it's okay. We all make up the world together." That was my approach.

I wish I could say there will only be one such incidence when you need to be strong. Certainly, some of my strength is part of my character, part of my personality, but it's taken me quite a long way. There have been so many times when I have realized that it's just me. I am the one responsible for my actions. I'm the one who will really determine if I'm successful or not. It won't be the pleading of my parents; it won't be the coaching of my friends; it's just me. It's just me! And I am responsible for me.

They say, the experts, of course, "No one can really make you happy." I believe that. I know when I am happy, vibrant, and full of energy, people around me are lifted a little bit. I know when I come in grumbling, people around me will grumble. They become disturbed and uncomfortable, so I've made a pact with myself to get up every day and be thankful for another day and to enjoy whatever that day has. My favorite saying when people complain is, "Things could always be worse." But I don't stop there. I would like to illustrate how things could be worse: You say you've got a flat tire? Well, you could have been shot today. Didn't pass a test? You could have been kicked out of school. Your dog messed on the carpet? The dog could have been stolen. I can't afford to let life get me down because life is a gift, and life is short and, above all, it's temporary. I do not waste time crying over spilled milk. If you spilled milk, clean it up. It's gone. Do I have regrets about yesterday? Would I do anything differently? I don't know. I have one life to live, as far as I know, and I have to live it. I believe that today is like an extraordinary present. That's what it is. Yesterday is a memory, and tomorrow may not come. I don't have time for that. I do enjoy life the way it is, and simple things, to me, are the most pleasurable.

Sense of self. I've been heard saying, "I know who I am and I know whose I am." One of the best compliments I ever received, while doing my medical training, was from Dr. La

Salle Leffall, one of the most well known black cancer surgeons in the country. I was coming through Howard as a student, and I was extremely inquisitive, not only about medicine but also about the whole process of being a physician.

When I was rotating through surgery, I was certainly drawn to the pathology more than the procedures sometimes. I was left-handed, didn't really understand the right hand way of tying off the knots. I was drawn to pathology and wanted to see the process and understand the disease. One time I was late for a meeting with Dr. Lefall. I was escorting a patient through surgery, and they were removing a gallbladder. The gallbladder tore and spilled gallstones in the abdomen. What was to be a simple procedure ended up taking about seven hours. Now, for those of you who are not familiar with medicine, when you are a medical student, your most unfavorite job in surgery is the retractor. You stand there with this heavy instrument, and you clear the field so the surgeon can see what he is doing. It is laborious; it is very hard on your legs, but you stand there if you want to get a really, really good grade and see a lot. You stand there motionless for hours. I could have left the operative field and said, "I've got to get to my class," but I said, "No, I'm going to see this all the way through." My surgeon appreciated it, but when I got out, Dr. Lefall did not.

He called me in and said, "Why were you late?"

I said, "My patient needed me."

He basically gave me corrective action, and I accepted it, but later as I was finishing school, he said, "Young Dr. Carter, you have the personality of a surgeon. Pretty good for a non-surgeon, I must say." I took that as a compliment, and I thought it meant that I was strong, somewhat aggressive, and willing to go the line for my patient. To me, that was a great compliment, coming from Dr. Lefall, coming from a surgeon. Those are things that you do when you think you are right, and you base your decisions on how you think you would like to be treated. I thought it was the right thing to do to stay with that patient. I was the one who worked the patient up and told him I would be with him, and I was when he woke up.

Though some negative consequences resulted from my actions, I was able to justify my actions, my choice. I did what I would have wanted done to me. Is that a strong sense of self? Perhaps. Some might consider it a little foolish. Is it about bucking the system? Not entirely. Sometimes it's about asking the system, "Is this the way it has to be? Is all of this necessary?" Maybe it takes someone who sees things a little differently to make some changes. Part of that, I guess, is having a sense of self, a sense of your ability, a sense that you can develop with influence and guidance from others. In other words, I have a sense of self and knowing who I am and whose I am is the protective nature of my self-confidence. I say to myself in the mirror when I greet myself every morning, "Good morning, Self. How are you?" And I smile sweetly because I'm smiling at me.

As I prepare to go into the office every day, I remind myself that I need to like myself. I do not go to work to be liked. I did not go to school to be liked. I did not go to school to be popular. I felt then as I do now. It is my opinion of me that counts. If I go to work today and I do my best, I've done a good job. If I go to work today and I do my best and I make some mistakes, I've done a good job. If I go to work today, do my best, make some mistakes, make some people angry, but I've done my best that I could do, I have done a good job. I realize that I will make some mistakes and I hope to gain knowledge from my mistakes. I hope to do better the next time. I hope not to repeat my mistakes, but I'm not going to beat myself up if I've made a mistake. I'm going to take corrective action.

Young people feel as if they have failed when they make a mistake. Dr. Leffall said, "The one diagnosis you will fail to make is the one you don't think about and the one that you don't know about. Surely if you don't know about it, it's difficult. If you don't think about it, then you are not exercising your brain to the full extent of its capacity." I made a note to myself to try to remember every pearl of wisdom my attendings gave to me, and I remember his words when I learn something new. I remember them because I want to improve. I don't want to not know of, or forget to think about, something that would help me help a patient. So you must be self-forgiving and self-loving. It is a continuous process because you will find yourself saying, "Oh, I could have done that better. Why did I do that?" My attitude is, "Do better next time."

A sense of self has been extremely helpful in furthering my career because I had to be forgiving of myself. For example: I believe so much in the "here and now" and so little in the "yesterday" that I constantly keep moving forward. When I was in high school, college, and even medical school, I would study, study, study, and study some more for the test.

Then I would take the test. Some of my friends, after the examination, would gather around and discuss what they thought they got wrong. I distanced myself from those people. In my mind, the test was over, the answer sheets were turned in, and I just had to wait for the score. I could not lament on Friday night about the test I took Friday morning. That was over. I noticed people would do that all the time, and they would kind of stay down. They couldn't release their minds to get ready for the next test. There was always going to be a next test. I wanted to say, "It's over. Do better next time. Learn from your mistakes. Don't rehash it."

Maybe parents can stress to their children that there are ways of studying, there are ways of keeping your self-confidence up, and after surviving and successfully completing so many standardized examinations, I feel that I am somewhat of an expert. I feel that these particular tests, in some ways, not only test one's knowledge but also one's perseverance. Sometimes I look around when I'm taking a test or monitoring a test, and I see the people showing defeat on their face. I always want to run over and say, "Take a break, go to the restroom, look at yourself in the mirror and tell yourself you can do it.

Don't let a piece of paper tell you you can't do it." That's self-preservation. That's a sense of self. We all need one badly.

I have further come to understand that a lot of test taking may not be explicitly cultural in the content, but in the manner. Having a strong sense of self is very important. Developing a strong sense of self entails somebody telling you know that you are okay as you, that you are loved as you, and that if you make a mistake, you will be still be you. For every piece of cloth, every thread that makes up the color, there is a unique purpose. I hope that we as adults, no matter what walk of life we choose, will pass this on to our children, to our students, and to our young people. It's okay to be a little different, that the person in the mirror, that reflection, should be smiling back when you smile at it. That's the only way we are going to pass it on.

Yes, I know who I am and whose I am. I know how I feel about tomorrow. It's from an old tapestry, deep within, and I hope I can pass it on to some of you reading this passage.

What Does Learning To Be Female Mean?

What do I mean when I say, "We have to learn to love being female?" I make this statement frequently when I am talking to young women or women's groups. What does it mean to learn to love being female? It means that today, at the turn of the century, there is still racism and sexism on the job, in the home, and in society. I have long bemoaned the color choices given to the infant, pink or blue, nothing in between. It seems for some, if you are female, you are supposed to be delicate, seen, and not heard. It's not fair. It doesn't allow us to become all that we can be.

There are attempts to form the woman's mind very early in life regarding what it is to be a female. The first is our shape, our figure. Young girls are encouraged to strive to maintain a certain figure or dress size, one that's unattainable. To be judged by how pretty you are as a little girl can give you a warped sense of self-esteem. The pressure to fit in, to be popular, is done differently for little girls: beauty contests at an early age, hair straighteners, hair styles. And if, somehow, you don't feel that you live up to the standard, you can end up not liking being a girl, not liking being a woman.

By the same token, our culture also says that once we reach thirty-five or forty, we are over the hill. Says who? I reject the notion that my hair cannot turn a naturally beautiful silver gray. Does that mean I'm over the hill? Should I put on deadly chemicals to change the color? Who is going to tell me that 40 is over the hill? Men are just considered mature. Whose standard is that? What is it that says I have to starve myself to maintain a certain size or to wear clothes that may be unbecoming at certain ages? You have to learn to love being female and to develop your own standards of beauty, to complement your common sense in how you dress your body in the work place and at play. I fear for little girls now when I listen to some of the pop songs on the radio or see some of the videos, particularly videos depicting African-American women or young ladies, where the outfits would have them arrested in no time for soliciting prostitution on the street. Some of these videos show girls bucking their buttocks at the camera, wearing nothing at all. What is this teaching our girls? They are learning that they will not be looked at more seriously when they are dressed, that they can't be attractive without showing cleavage.

We have to learn to love being female! We have to change the standard. Now, I have already talked about hair, and there is nothing wrong with getting hair done, but sometimes I see young women paying hundreds of dollars to get their hair braided, and their children aren't being fed or they need assistance for their utilities. Some women have bought the old myth that length of hair defines femininity. It can be harmful to see the ads for the prettiest little girl because they always show only one standard of beauty. What about the other little girls? What does that mean for those who do not look the same way? How about the distorted image of intelligent girls. Thick glasses? Unattractive? What is unattractive? Now is the time for women to say, "Hey, that's not right." We have to set new standards for ourselves. We have to accept each other and I think it takes a lot of strength in today's world to accept being a woman, living as a woman. We must stop society from preventing us from bonding together on a deeper level. We have to set our standards.

I decided a long time ago that I was going to do what was comfortable for me, and I guess Mother Nature played a role. Because of my sensitive skin, I cannot wear a lot of makeup, nor would I. It's not practical in what I do. It is more practical for me to wear my hair short, as I need to wash it often and I like to be athletic. I like to work out; it's good for my mind, body, and soul. I made up my mind that I was going to confront and appreciate my reflection in the mirror. I was not going to let a designer dress me and tell me what I should be wearing. Oh, I used to do that. I remember when I didn't have a lot of disposable income I would try to find a way to buy new clothes every week to meet that expectation. One day, I said, "This is ridiculous. If it fits and it looks good to me, I'm going to wear it as long as it's in good condition. I'm not going to fall for that." I'm a firm believer that our minds tell us when we look good and when we don't.

I don't need a name on my clothes. I have one; it's Joye Carter. I don't need someone's name on the back pocket of my jeans. I have a name! I'm not going to pay money for that. I'm comfortable with who I am. I'm comfortable growing older. I tease my female friends about being fine at forty, fine at fifty, and fine at sixty. Why not? It's called loving yourself, not being put into a box. Sure, being a woman is wonderful. I would not want to be anything else. There is no question that when I walk into a room, I am a woman! But if one judges my skills and capabilities *just* on the way I look, one will have missed the most important part of the book by glancing only at the cover. It's about learning to love being a woman. That's something our society must nurture. For me, it meant adapting in a white male-oriented profession. I never intended to blend in. It's never going to happen. I'm not going to apologize for my skin color, the kinkiness of my hair, or for my gender. I will celebrate it. I will show through my actions and work that there is no difference in my end product. It's about learning to love being female.

There are many things I can't do and I acknowledge them. I don't let anyone say to me, "You can't do that because you are a woman. Or women just don't do that." Let me find out for myself. I don't want to put myself in danger, but why not challenge myself? It's about learning to love being female! It has been a great boost for me to see women in all fields and men in non-traditional roles. We need to be moving ahead in this society. Don't get me wrong. There is nothing wrong with being a caretaker, and males <u>and</u> females can do that. To put people into boxes in which they do not fit, just because of their gender or their age, doesn't make sense. The brain drain is what occurs when we take people and say, "Okay, you are a certain age, and you have to leave this job." Why not judge them on their performance? Love yourself!

Now, surely, you are not going to wear a mini-skirt and a string of pearls when climbing up a telephone pole for a repair job. Learn what's appropriate. Educate yourself on what the job is that you are after before you go for the interview. Have faith in your skills and yourself. I love being female. I wouldn't have it any other way. I have learned.

Aren't You Afraid?

Many times after giving scientific lectures or when I appear on a professional panel with my white male colleagues, I am asked the question "Aren't you afraid? Sometimes I chuckle to myself because I know this question is asked out of ignorance, usually from media persons. Other people ask because they are generally concerned about how I deal with death on a daily basis. I have to answer according to what audience I am addressing.

Many times people view me as a woman, or as a young woman, or as a black young woman, and they forget that my title is *Chief* Medical Examiner. I explain to them that if I was afraid of what I was doing, I would not have made it to this point in my career. I also have to explain that in reality, with the exception of diseases that can be transmitted through the dead body, I don't really have a lot to fear. I point out that we need to be fearful of those who walk around us. I have always been comfortable with a dead body. Much of this comfort is based in my spirituality.

There really is no need of fear. Life is circular, beginning and ending with birth and death. For me, that's not a big issue. It's something that I have always been comfortable with, and I feel that's how I knew I was going to be successful in this chosen field. I don't have the same outlook most people have. When mother tells me that somebody we knew and loved has died, I say, "Mother, there is no need to grieve over that person because they're gone." She cannot understand this. We have to help the people who are left behind to carry on without their loved ones.

There is another way of analyzing this question. I get this accusatory tone from the media: "Well, aren't you afraid?" I interpret this as a sexist question. I say, "You pass up the white males who are also engaged in death investigation and approach me. Frankly, I probably have more nerve than most men out there walking around when it comes to handling a dead body." Certainly, I have seen the most gruesome and sometimes unimaginable crimes and outcomes of violent and tragic accidents. It's really difficult to comprehend how the human body can be blown up into small pieces, or how the face can simply be removed, or how one human being could do some of these horrible acts to another person. These are chilling thoughts, but I must accept the responsibility of documenting death. It should not make a difference whether a male or female is capable if they are handling the requirements of the job.

I say to students who ask, "How do you handle this?" You have to know why you are doing it. We do have to learn detached professionalism. What does that mean? If you are so upset by what you are seeing, you cannot give your full attention to documenting that person's death. If you cannot bear to see the effects of tremendous burning or chemical deaths or poisonings or even gunshot wounds, you cannot document what has happened to that person. You also cannot go back and help the family through this tragedy. I counsel families in this profession, grief counseling, and help survivors realize that they can go on with their lives. A medical examiner MUST be able to confront and deal with these issues; therefore, this profession may not be for everybody.

Seeing what I have seen for the last twenty-some years has made me more respectful of human life. I tell people I love and care about them often. I say to people, "Don't talk about me when I'm in the ground because I won't be in the ground. Those will be my remains." I'm very careful about those words. I mean them and I repeat them in the community. You can't be so afraid of death that you don't live every day; you should live every day to the fullest. Daily, I notice the simple parts life, take time to "smell the coffee," to appreciate somebody. It's terrible to have people say all these wonderful accolades at a funeral when they didn't say them before that person died. I hear families say, "You know, I wish I hadn't had that fight." I have developed a motto: *Don't go to bed angry; don't leave the house angry; don't sweat the small stuff. Is it really that important?*

I ask young students, "If you knew you wouldn't see that person any more, would you just make the comment that you just made? Would you really do that?" Most people cannot accept their inevitable death, at least usually not until they get up into the late thirties. However, we have very, very young people who have exposed to death in a way that I really can't imagine. As a child, I experienced death when my grandparent died, but I was very far removed. My curiosity about death led me into the field of science and medicine, but I did not have a personal experience as young children are having today, for example, like being exposed to the bodies of homicide victims. I wonder what will be the outcome in the years that pass of youth who discover a dead body, either in their home or on their way home from school. What will be the impact? If you are professionally trained and if you have enough confidence in your abilities, you should not have fear. For those who ask if I am afraid merely because I am a woman, then I tell them to wise up. This is not a womanly or manly thing. It's about people. The ultimate goal of my profession is to document a person's death. Death knows no gender; it knows no socioeconomic level barrier; it knows no ethnic group, and it knows no age. Death is something that we have to come to grips with if we are going to be in this field and if we are going to assist people through the process.

It is difficult to perform a postmortem examination on an acquaintance or friend, but sometimes, at the chief level, it happens. One experience took an emotional toll on me. While working in Washington, D.C., one of my own employees from the medical examiner's office was killed. The law clearly stated that the responsibility of the Office of the Chief Medical Examiner of the District of Columbia was to investigate homicides. When the employee was killed, it was a traumatic event for everybody in my office. I was at a meeting in San Antonio, Texas, and had just arrived the night before when I got the news. I left immediately. The employee was a gentleman who had died secondary to domestic violence. My entire staff was shaken to the core. I could not, because of the law, call in the federal authorities or those from my prior military experience to investigate or perform the examination. I had his body moved to a nearby hospital where I personally conducted the autopsy. It was a traumatic event. What I had to do was pray. I had to pray before I started because I needed that emotional strength. I got on my knees, and I asked God to give me the strength to deal with the situation because I knew the alleged perpetrator as well. I had to step outside of myself, turn on my scientific automatic pilot, and do the best job that I could do to document this man's death.

I was extremely fond of this employee. He was one of my autopsy assistants, and he was a very nice person. The injuries he suffered were significant, destroying his face and damaging other parts of his torso. It was a very emotionally and physically trying procedure. One other staff member who did not know the deceased assisted me. We did the examination with the help of the hospital staff. It was important that this be done away from the medical examiner's office because of the effect on the other staff. There is nothing that is more hurtful than when it is one of your own. That's when it really hits home.

After I completed the examination. I was exhausted, truly exhausted, in a way that is hard to explain. All I could do after that examination was sit for a little while. Then I called my grandmother who had been a source of inspiration my entire life. When I told her about my ordeal, she simple said, "You have to do your best, no matter what. Didn't you take an oath to do that?" She said, "I got to be my age by doing what I knew I had to do and doing it the best way that I could do it." Now this woman did not have a formal education, but she always managed to teach me something. I got strength from her words. And I still remember the injuries on this man. I did not have nightmares; instead, I remember his laughter and practical jokes, even the type of food he ate. I will never forget this, but I have developed special coping skills that allow me to go on from day to day.

I do the best for the body. I know that the person, his or her soul or life force, has passed on to another place. So, in a round about way, no, I am not afraid of the dead body. I have to respect the dead body. We haven't touched on the fact that we have to be aware as medical people that certain diseases can be transmitted via blood or tissue, even from the dead. There is a thick line between respecting the dead body and making fun of the dead body in order to become comfortable. Many people who tour the medical examiner's office are not medical professionals, and they usually make jokes, laughing, saying things like, "Give me a hamburger or whatever." I quickly put a stop to that. That's not respectful, and I say to them honestly, "If that was your loved one, if that was your mother, your father, your sister or brother, or your child, would you want people coming through like you laughing?" It sobers them. I have been blessed with the innate ability to look at everybody who comes through there. No matter what they looked like or what part of town they lived in, I stop and remember that I would want my loved one to be treated with respect and dignity. You really shouldn't fear what you understand. Education, experience, and job fulfillment lead me away from fear toward competence and peace.

How Do You Cope With
Negative Media Portrayals?

Another question I am frequently asked is "How do you cope with negative media coverage?" The answer is complex, and I want to explain thoroughly. I feel that the media has a job to do, and I have a job to do, and they are not the same job. I go back to what my grandmother told me years ago: "If you weren't doing something right, they wouldn't be talking about you." In this position as a medical examiner, I have a certain amount of power to make decisions, to be truthful no matter what. So the media is interested in me.

I am often quoted, saying, "The medical examiner's office is one that people love to hate." Again, people fear what they don't understand. We, in general and as insignificant human beings, would love to know why we die and how to stop it, but, in reality, we don't and we can't. We don't know when or where, and that's the mystique and mystery of death. We often think people die unfairly or untimely, but we can't control that. So, when you devote your life to studying and documenting death, you become part of that fear.

Because I am a black woman and one of the few females to lead a busy urban medical examiner office, I am good material for the media coverage. Also, despite the fact that it is not a political position, it runs arm in arm with politicians. Certain deaths are political, such as deaths of individuals who are in police custody or individuals who die because something went wrong in the hospital. These issues are relatively non-important to the greater masses, yet through the manipulation of journalists, they become a front page item. Because we as medical examiners are to be neutral fact-finders and we are not to have the burden of constituency appeal to us like elected coroners do, we become a voice to be reckoned with. I say often, "I am not a person who is going to yield to pressure." A lot of people want to try me, and they realize I will not yield to pressure. I try to do the right thing, as I know it, day in and day out. That means making unpopular decisions.

I'm also quoted as saying, "The media should not run a death investigation." And I mean that quite seriously. I will stand up to that. For the most part, one's opinion of me is simply that: one's opinion. I have a high opinion of myself. I have enough love for myself that when I go to work every day, I'm not there to seek love. I'm there to do my job. I know who

I am. I know whose I am. And I know whose power I bow to. It is not the journalists. I have enough self-confidence and enough self-worth and enough belief in God to protect me, no matter what. People would love to see me bent and distraught and sad and mopey, but mere words cannot inflict long-lasting harm. I know it bothers some people that I don't show those signs of weakness, but I come from strong stuff. And, as a black woman who is the granddaughter and great-granddaughter of women who have been through much more, this is but a puddle I have to step over.

The odd thing is when I moved into the position as a medical examiner, into a situation where I took over for someone who had been there for a long time, I was bound to make changes. In general, people don't like to change, and therefore, I had to be strong enough to push those changes in some ways. Once people see change as inevitable, they accept it, shunning the old way. You have to be visionary; you have to see things as they can be and imagine them. The word "can't" is a word that I was told as a very small child not to use because there is nothing you cannot do if it makes sense and if you put your mind and your heart into doing it.

I don't fret about the media, and, I must say, that in Houston, Texas, I laugh about it. But I think it's a crime, in a city this large with only one major newspaper, to see manipulation of the facts. And they get away with it. I have received probably more than my fair share of negative coverage for a large number of reasons in Houston. Certainly, some of it comes from the way I look and the way I work. As one reporter told me, there's no story to report on positive things. People can come to my shop and see for themselves.

I stated to the media when I first arrived in Houston that I expected a challenge and would meet the challenge because I can do good things. But how do I deal with it? I really don't. It's their job to report the news or what they perceive as news. It's my job to investigate death. The one thing I have always tried to do is educate the media, which is sometimes a very difficult thing to do. I constantly say that there is no coroner's office in Houston, Texas, nor has there been for over forty-some years. We give them the facts, and that's their job. It is amazing that the media can write a front-page story, and if they do write a retraction, it's very small and buried somehow within the minor part of the paper. That's what the media does. I don't fault them; I certainly don't waste time getting angry over it because, as far as I'm concerned, anger is an emotion that takes a lot of energy, and I don't waste my energy on insignificant things. My energy is for me.

If you play only to the media in hopes they will give you great coverage, you will fail. You may not like me, you certainly won't know me, but in the end you will respect the job I do. I tell the media as I tell the families, "I do the same thing for you that I would do for my own family." I resist the media's attempt to sensationalize certain crimes because the decedent's family is victimized all over again. It is disgusting to see the media push a microphone into someone's face and say, "How does it feel to have your loved one die this way?" The media disrespects mourning, an important and healthy process. I don't believe in sensationalizing in order to sell papers or headline the evening news. There have been some very sad outcomes of that happening.

When I worked in D.C., a woman was found in the lion's den of the national zoo. She had been attacked and partially consumed by the lions. It immediately became a media frenzy. This woman's identity was not known and not only were we trying to figure out how she had been killed, but who she was. We had a lot of issues going on at one time:

Number one, identifying the victim. Number two, this was the national zoo. Number three, should the lions that attacked her be put to death? As we were working up the case, thinking we were working quietly to identify her, to notify her next of kin first, one of the reporters from a local station got one of the police investigators to tell her who the person was. Before we could notify the next of kin, who were in another part of the country and knew nothing about this, the woman's name and identity were announced on the evening news, nationwide, for her small, minor children to view. This is how they found out that their mother was dead. It was really unconscionable. I held a press conference and I asked the media, "If that was your loved one, what would you want me to do? Would you want to know or hear the grizzly description of her death on the evening news?" When it becomes personal, people in the media deal with it in a completely different manner. But when it's just a job, they really don't think about who they hurt.

We also struggled to decide if these animals should be killed. We spent an interesting week actually watching the animals defecate to see which part of the body had been consumed. We drained the mote in the lion's den. I had learned a lot about lions and knew that lions don't generally go into the water. We were able to reconstruct the entire scene after we drained the mote, and we found out that this young woman, who was apparently mentally ill, had climbed up the wall on her own, sat there for awhile, leaving prints, and then jumped into the pit. We could see the lions' claw prints in the silt and how far out they had gone into the water. It was finally decided that the animals had only done what nature had intended for them to do, and they were allowed to live.

The media is a double-edged sword. It can be very useful or it can be very hazardous. You have to know what you are dealing with.

I have received probably the most nefarious comments from the main newspaper in Houston, Texas, due to changes and to a few disgruntled employees. That has not stopped the success of the office. But, at the same time, because of the continuous coverage that I have received, the paper succeeded in not only *not* making me a villain but making me one of the most popular and prayed for administrators in Harris County, Texas. There is hardly a day that goes by that someone does not stop me, having recognized me from my picture in some negative article, and say "We're pulling for you; we're praying for you; we know what you're doing, keep doing it and please don't leave." I have had letters and hugs from every ethnic group in Houston, and I must thank the media for that.

So, how do I deal with the media coverage? I take each day as it comes. I do my best every day. When I get up in the morning, I pray to God to thank Him for another day. I remember that He's the one in charge, He's the one I bow to, and He truly has mapped out my life. When I get bad press, it's just bad press. I have enough confidence to do what the job requires, and I've got very, very broad shoulders. Just lay it on; it's not going to weigh me down. It is very important, I think, for younger people to understand that. People have to know why they are doing what they are doing, to recognize that every day is not going to be pleasant; every day is not going to be perfect; every day is not going to be successful. Roll with the punches. Learn from mistakes. Admit when you could have done a better job, and try your best. That's all that I can do. There is someone else in charge of my life, and it's not the media.

The media can sometimes be a wonderful tool if you can harness some of that positive energy. Imagine what it was like fifty years ago when we didn't have the general use of the computer, of the Internet, of mass TV. We would have lost a lot of information. I think you have to take the good with the bad. Media is a way of informing the masses. And with that, it can be a tool to educate as well. I do try to use the media when I feel there is important information that needs to get out to the public. For example, a particular chemical or drug is becoming popular, we need to educate those who are responsible for young people or those who might encounter a person using this drug and not understand his/her behavior, such as law enforcement, parents, or college administrators. Medical examiners put out certain warnings because we see cyclic and repetitive deaths that occur year in and year out because someone did not get the message, such as not leaving infants in the tub, or not letting toddlers around five-gallon buckets filled with liquid. The media can educate the public.

I have, for many years, used the media to distribute positive and correct information about organ and tissue donation procedures. So, certainly, if you respect the job the media has to do, and remember that they don't do what you do, you can get some things accomplished. As for the negative outcomes, again, it can't be all that negative if they're talking about it. You will always weather those storms if you believe in yourself and in the mission that you are here to accomplish.

Why Do You Describe Yourself As Armed And Dangerous?

I have used that expression a number of times. It gets the attention of my audience. They may first think, "here's a black woman who is probably carrying a weapon." That's as wrong as it can be. I want to let young people know that they can be "armed and dangerous" in a very unique way. You see, I describe myself as "armed and dangerous" meaning, I am armed with knowledge and I am dangerous because I have the confidence to use that knowledge at will. I often say, "I can slay somebody verbally without shedding a tear or a drop of blood." It's an acquired confidence from being able to learn, to read, and to appreciate my environment. I don't have to go into a meeting shouting, kicking, and screaming, using foul language, or intimidating somebody with physical strength. I can get my point across in a way that will make you think about issues. I can say exactly what I mean. I can back up what I say with the literature, with the history, and before you know it, you have fallen to my power. The power of education! I think we can raise an army of people just like me with the strength of character to do what's right, to have a moral obligation to neighbors, and to let others know that they need to come prepared for battle.

When I stand up to say something, whether it be a statement or a question, I am confident in my abilities to make myself heard. I don't have to be the loudest one in the room. Now, I haven't always been that comfortable with speaking, but I learned and developed self-confidence while in high school. My knowledge has increased, and I learned to think and make decisions. It's something that young people today need to be encouraged to do. Many times when I'm out talking with the public or when I go to schools and talk to students, I see how many of the students want to ask a question but are afraid to do so. Somehow they have learned that because they don't know something, it's bad. They also have learned that it's not okay to ask a question. Many times young people, and adults, will avert their gaze when speaking to me. They won't look me in the eyes. We have to learn to make eye contact. When I look you in the eye, I get a feel for whether or not you understand what I am saying. I see people fidgeting when they have something to say, talking more with their hands than with their mouths. It's distracting. It muddles their message. Unfortunately, I see many of our leaders who don't have reading skills, and this, many times, takes away from the message they are trying to give. For me, it's good to be "armed and dangerous." It's a comfortable advantage, and it's an advantage that everybody could have.

I preach a lot about the need for education. Early education is the one way to become "armed and dangerous" in the good sense. You have got to start the kids *early*. As a child, I was always asked what I wanted to do when I grew up. Always. And it wasn't enough to say I didn't know. I was shown examples from people visiting my school and Officer Friendly, the nurse. We were taken to museums, we were instructed to read and learn and to ask questions. We couldn't just say, "I am not sure." We had to think of something. That encouraged me to explore many types of professions. It made me learn, and it made me feel that there were so many things I could do as a child growing up in the sixties and seventies.

All of these concepts are part of the fabric, of the quilt. All these threads come together. I knew I wanted to help other people. We need to know that this kind of battle can be won, and it doesn't have to be at a premium. We can be "armed and dangerous" and shoot bullets of truth in the heart of the enemy.

Is Your Father A Doctor?

Another frequently asked question from my colleagues in medicine is "Is your father a physician?" I always smile when I hear it. Of course, my father was not a physician. Thank God, I would probably not have gone into this field. I very proudly say, "Oh no, my father was not a physician. He was a mason. He made brick for a living, and he could do anything to a house with his hands." I always add, "That's why I live in a brick house today. My father taught me about brick. He taught me about life, helping me to realize that it's not necessary to do exactly what one's parents did, nor is there any shame in what my parents did." My father was a strong man, and I always had a sense that he loved what he did. He passed that on to me. Where did you come from? How did you get into this field? How could you possibly have developed this interest without any other physicians in the family? These are other interpretations of this question. My father encouraged me to do what I wanted, as long as I did it honestly.

I owe some things to my father, which differ from what I owe to my mother. I was the youngest of four girls. I was the last hope. I think the reason my mother named me Joye is because I was going to be the last child. They had tried five times to have a boy. Apparently, there was a child in between me and my older sister who did not survive and who would have been a male child. I knew this, and I really tried my hardest to be the little tomboy that my father never had, and he supported my athletic side, that curious side that kind of got me into trouble with my mother a little bit. Back in the neighborhood when I was very small, I was the tomboy. I didn't have a whole lot of use for frilly dolls. I would cut their hair and be bored with them. I always wanted a Tonka truck. I loved getting in the dirt and mud and climbing trees, and my father allowed me to do that, with a warning to behave, of course. I recall following him on a tour of the brickyard one day, and he showed me how they made brick. And I loved it! He was such a strong, athletic man. All of his brothers had been football heroes in the little town where I was born, and he had this Herculean physique that I always admired. He also had a nurturing side, and although he was rough on the outside, he was very, very tender, a pushover. I used to follow him on some of his part-time jobs, and I would watch him take a house that was falling down, restructure it, and make steps and stairs. I still remember fondly wanting to have a brick barbecue pit made because he had made those in people's yards, and they were so beautiful to me.

My father was a medic in the Army doing the Korean War, and maybe this contributed to my desire to be a doctor. My father taught me to act sincerely; he guided me. I was independent as a child. I wanted my own money; I wanted to be in control of my own destiny.

When I was too young to go to school, my sisters and I did not receive any allowance whatsoever. My parents basically said that it was a privilege for us to live with them. So I would collect soda pop bottles from the neighbors and take them back to the store to get that little refund, which added up to quite a few pennies. I would save my money if I needed to buy something that my parents wouldn't get for me. Later on, when I really wanted to get into books and more activities, I decided I needed a real job. In the fifth grade, I applied to become the first papergirl in my town. Some people were shocked. It was a good job, the hours were good, and since I was in the fifth grade there was really nothing else I could do to earn money. I wasn't into babysitting. So I applied to deliver the East Liverpool Review, and I got the job. My father helped me. He showed me how to hoist that bag, weighing about 20 pounds, over my shoulder, and he taught me how to fold the paper so it would fly through the air and glide onto the steps. On cold days or holidays, he would get up early with me in the mornings and help me deliver papers.

Something else I owe to my father is my love of coffee. When dad would go to the brickyard, he had wonderful working hours from six in the morning until one in the afternoon. I would get up in the morning and creep downstairs, and he would be up already and getting ready for work. He used a lot of milk and a lot of sugar in his coffee; it was a certain color, and I would peep around and watch him get ready, and I would sip the coffee out of the saucer. That is one reason I wanted to drink coffee as a little girl. When I was reaching puberty, I had a growth spurt. I was considered tall, taller than my classmates, and I had big feet. I had heard someone say that if you drank coffee it would stunt your growth. I wanted to slow my growth down, so I would sip on his coffee, and I loved it even though when I grew into myself and began to like who I was, I stopped drinking coffee. But amazingly, when I was in medical school and my father died, I started drinking coffee again and haven't stopped since. Every time I fix my coffee with lots of cream and, of course, now I use a little sugar, I think about my dad. I think about that coffee cup always spilling over into the saucer, slurping that saucer of coffee. I think of my father's strength. I always have a little bit of him every time I drink coffee.

I would never want to be the kind of person that creates an imaginary family. My father was a laborer, and he loved what he did. He was a union man, and his union worked for him. This fact keeps me grounded enough to remember that whatever I do, if I like it and do it well, I am blessed. Like brick, my father gave me a strong foundation. He was not a physician, but a healer nonetheless.

Who Are Your Role Models?

This type of question always makes me pause. I don't think I give the answer most people are looking to hear. There are many people who have been role models and mentors for my development. My ancestors are my mentors, people I have never known and have never seen. They are the Africans who survived the middle passage to raise families under the most subversive criminal system in this country's history: to those Native Americans on one side of my family who I will never know, to the black people who struggled to survive and became educated when it was a crime to do so, to those who fought for our civil rights. All of these ancestors are my primary role models. When people give me praise and applaud my accomplishments, it's because someone has come before me who cleared the way, who made it possible for me to achieve what I have. Those people exhibited a strength of character that I don't think I could come close to possessing. The African men and women who were removed from their homeland and brought to this country have to be role models. Those who survived that treacherous trip, landed in this country, and survived are my examples of strength. When I think of how far

American blacks have come since the end of slavery, it's really amazing that so many people have now achieved wonderful elements of the American dream, and yet who, just a little over one hundred years ago, were treated less than animals.

I keep reminders in my home and around my work desk of these people who are nameless and faceless. I was blessed to purchase brass chains that were used to enslave little girls in West Africa. These beautiful, solid brass, extremely heavy bracelets are a stark reminder of what happened and what could happen again lest we forget. I have also been able to obtain leg irons that were used for the male Africans. It's a constant reminder of what our society has done to continue to enslave the black male.

I was given a beautiful, hand-made doll. This doll was made by an old black woman on a roadside in Florida. The body is really a two-liter soda bottle with a hand-made dress, black skin, and a round figure. I purposely keep her in my house, in my dining room overlooking my table, and I call her Aunt Kizzie. Aunt Kizzie looks like the sterotypical black female figure of the 1930s and 1940s, as portrayed on TV, with a large bandana around her head and very dark skin - - a pleasant round woman. To me, this is the enduring characterization of the black female who, in this country, in America, had the strength to mother others as well as her own children. That's a whole lot of love! That's a whole lot of caring by one person. This doll embodies those women. I keep this doll to remind me of the strong black women. There are many black women I have embraced as individual role models. Today, I take this doll out with me when I'm speaking to young people to let them know that they should never hang their heads and be embarrassed by stereotypes, but to see the good in them and move forward. This is my first set of role models, and they are always a part of my spirit.

My second set of role models were my immediate family, starting from my grandmothers who taught me so many different things about life, God, and how to treat other people. My maternal grandmother, Momma Hart, was not only my grandmother but also my best friend growing up. My grandmother taught me about life. I learned from her. We were literally soulmates, I always thought. She taught me to tell the truth and how easy it is to tell the truth and how difficult it is to lie. I learned from her. I don't know why, but there were many times when I would not accept another person's word unless my grandmother, in her own way, showed me what was right.

Many of the lessons she taught me have stayed with me throughout my entire life.

The earliest one that I remember was when I was a little girl. My mother would always take us out to visit my grandmother at least once a week and we all got to know her. But during one summer, I stayed with her for a week. I actually was getting a little bored because there were no little kids around for me to play with, and I was keeping myself entertained by playing with her knick knacks. My grandmother had collections of ceramic deer and all kinds of salt and pepper shakers, and being true to my animal loving form, I was playing with a little set of deer and I knocked one over. I remember thinking, "Oh well, she's old. She can't hear that."

But she heard a little crash and said, "What was that?"

I said, "Oh, nothing." And I put the little broken deer back up on the shelf, moved away, and hoped she wouldn't see it. I never knew she saw it while I was there, but when my mother arrived on Sunday to take me home, a few hours later my grandmother called. I cringed because I knew exactly what it was about.

She spoke with my mother first; then my mother called me to the phone, and all my grandmother said was, "You know, when you tell one lie, you've got to keep on telling it. When you tell the truth, you only have to say it once, and you can say it the same way all the time." I was terrified that she would be angry with me. I apologized, and I cried, and the next day my mother and I went out and bought her a new set of ceramic salt and peppershakers. For many years after that, I always gave her salt and pepper shakers. But I never forgot that lesson. This was one of the many things she taught me about respecting myself and treating everybody the same way. She was just, again, my soulmate. Even though she wasn't a particularly educated woman, she was loaded with common sense and love, and I think a lot of my character comes from my grandmother. There were ways she could get me to do what no one else could. She was definitely a role model.

I learned other things from my paternal grandmother. We weren't as close as Momma Hart and I, but I have a lot of admiration for her. I recall, as a child, that this was a strong black woman who bore her husband sixteen children, and she worked as a housekeeper all of her life, way up into her seventies. Every summer she would take her grandchildren to the shoe store, and we would all get a new pair of Hushpuppies. Now back then, those weren't particularly my favorite shoes, but it was just so admirable that this lady would be able to get shoes for all of her grandchildren, and, looking back now, I think that was just such a wonderful thing to do. These are lessons learned that I think have placed me in a position far beyond my years. In another sense, the management, the care and the respect of other people has promoted me throughout my profession.

My next level of role models would have to be my parents, my mother and father who, through their blending together, gave me different characteristics that have helped me find my way and they, individually, have shown me other pathways. To my mother, especially, for her love of literature, art, education, and her sense of style. To my father for his love of sports and his encouragement to me to be my best, his strength, and his love of the simple things. To both my parents for that extra heavy dose of stubbornness that I got from each one.

My other role models are my mother and father who, each in his and her own way, gave me gifts from each of them that went into my physical and emotional makeup. My father worked with his hands and loved the earth and the simple life. I admired his physical prowess. My mother, with her literature, education, art, and her sense of style, formed me.

Another role model/mentor was Dr. Davis, the gentleman who mentored me from across the country without knowing me but cared enough to help a young person pursue a dream. He never ridiculed me. He always treated me with respect and always encouraged me to ask "why," and to stay involved with the community. We have in common the love of gospel singing, particularly Mahalia Jackson. I look at this man and see him as such an humble person who can walk into a room and talk to anybody. Here is a man with a building named after him, still well thought of around the world, yet he has humility. He treats everybody well. He is a mentor worth emulating, and I have tremendous respect for him.

I have always had great admiration for the comedian Bill Cosby. My father bore a resemblance to Bill Cosby, and I was always very proud of that. I have always enjoyed comedy. I think a little levity is good for everybody. I grew up listening to Bill Cosby's albums about his childhood, and I followed his career as he continued to pursue his education. He is a human being with faults like everybody else, and he acknowledges those and keeps going. I do admire that.

Other role models are my many teachers, both in my general education, K through 12, in college, and my professors in medical school. Teaching is one of the most underrated, underpaid professions in this country, and I think it is a shame the way these individuals are abused. I hope that at some point we will move from sheer entertainment to focusing on the people who shape our children's future. These are our teachers.

I think the greatest role model for me is my spiritual guidance. It's something I cannot live up to, but I try. This is probably not what most people would say, but God is the giver of all things. I see His force daily, and there is nothing that compares.

Is Your Mother Proud of You?

This is usually posed as a statement, and, yes, my mother is very proud of me. She is a one woman PR firm, and I'm glad that she is proud. My upbringing has quite a bit to do with my profession, the love I have of my career, and the person I turned out to be.

I have mentioned before that I owe many traits to my mother, as well as my father. As mothers and daughters go, I always saw myself as an exact opposite of my mother. She was squeamish and never liked a lot of stress, and, of course, I was just the opposite. But my mother had some very wonderful characteristics that she passed on to me. For example, I always stand up for myself, and I make sure I am treated with respect, no matter what. As children, my mother would tell us, "Never leave that store without a bag and a receipt." Every now and then, one of my sisters would come home without those items, and my mother would say, "You go back and you get a bag and you get a receipt. Never leave without a bag and a receipt." That taught me, again, that basically the whole issue is respect and accountability. And, of course, we would never buy some penny candy with the change. You brought it all home. My mother did have a way of standing up for herself that I know I have fully embraced.

She also taught me strength of character. When I was in high school, I was driving my mother's car. It was big and green, and I always thought of it as a large alligator. My junior year, I drove this car to school some girlfriends. We were going to some after school activity, just talking and laughing and not paying attention. As I drove out of the parking lot, I hit one of my teacher's cars and all I heard was this big crunch and crack. Again, my mother's car was very large, and my teacher's car was not very big, more like a midsize car. I hit the fender right and broke the headlight. I was in shock! I was afraid of what would happen when I went home. But I went and told my mother what I had done. My friends were with me, and they were kind of waiting for my mother to lower the boom and lose her temper. She calmly said, "Go tomorrow and tell your teacher you did it and find out how much it will cost. We will pay for the light to be replaced." She didn't yell or scream, and I was slightly relieved. I said to myself, *Well, that's it. I won't be driving to school any more!*

I got up for school the next morning prepared to walk to school, which really wasn't that far away, and my mother said, "Where are you going?"

"I'm on my way to school."

"Oh, no, no, no. Take the keys."

I started to say, "But I just hit…"

She interrupted me. "You drive that car and show yourself you can drive and pay attention without hitting anybody." I was really afraid to drive the car because I had lost a little bit of confidence, but I did and everything was okay. I have never hit another car since then. That built my self-confidence and showed me that my mother supported me. I learned a big lesson. Mom and I definitely have different views on life, and I guess that's what families are all about. Nonetheless, she is a strong woman, definitely a strong woman, and I owe some of my strengths to her.

I am asked many times about how my mother feels about what I do, and it is hard to answer that question. I don't know if she fully comprehends everything that I do. She has asked many times to view an autopsy, but I discourage this because I know my mother. I know her real well. She is quite squeamish. I mean, she gets upset with the James Bond movies.

I don't think it is right for her to view an autopsy unless she has a good reason to.

My mother has been there, knowing part of what I do, and I think sometimes feeling the sting of the media much more that I do. When I was in the military and had to leave for a secret mission, I could not call and tell my mother that I was going away. I would just call and talk about any little thing because I knew she would just be on pins and needles until I returned and be very, very upset. To this date, it has never been a practice of mine to discuss my work with anybody, including my mother. I often say to my students and employees that one of my mottos is "trust no one." Even my mother wouldn't know these things. I just don't believe in sharing when it comes to the job or if it entails betraying someone else's trust. My mother knows that if I should learn of something that is negative about somebody, I'm not one to repeat it. Many times I just never want to hear it. I believe in peace in the home and peace after work.

So I guess she has helped me to become the me that I am. I think she recognized when I was a small child that I was a little bit different, even from my sisters. I used to tell her, "Mom, sometimes I think the stork really did drop me here and

I'm not related to the other girls." I didn't have the same personality or desires that my sisters had as far as the things that I chose to play with or the activities that I got involved with. I was quite a literal thinker even back then.

Now my mother is a wonderful cook. She loves to cook and cook for people and, of course, as mothers do, she cooks all the wrong things. She has always been a very serious baker; that kind of runs in her family. In the second or third grade, I was playing outside one summer day. The newscaster said, "It's hot enough to fry an egg." Well, I took that to heart. I wanted to see an egg fry on the sidewalk. So I ran into the kitchen and got one of my mother's good brown eggs, and I ran outside and threw it on the sidewalk. Of course, all it did was just kind of run all over the sidewalk into a gelatinous mess. Mom wasn't all that happy, but I guess she understood.

I used to get into mischief, just down right mischief, when I was a little girl because I was curious. I was curious about nature and science. I was fascinated with heat and electricity. I would take plastic and put it on a light bulb and turn the light on and listen to it snap, crackle, and pop as it melted and changed form. My father got very upset about this, and I tried to explain that I was doing a scientific experiment.

My parents gave me a stern warning that if I did it again, part of me would be a little tender. That's just part of growing up.

I tell my mother now playfully, "You know, when I was a little girl you would buy me these dolls and I never really wanted a lot of dolls. I had always wanted a Tonka truck. I would get tired of playing with dolls, and they were kind of fragile. Tonka trucks seemed to last forever, and I loved them. I also enjoyed playing with the dirt and the dump truck." So, of course, when I grew up I chose an SUV, which is what I have now. I told my mother, "You never got me one so I got my own Tonka truck." We always laugh about that.

My mother knows that she is not the only mother in my life, and I want to take this time to thank my other "mothers" for all that they have done for me. You see, I left home to go to college right out of high school at age eighteen, and I told my mother something that I know probably hurt her. As I was packing for college, I said to her, "This is the last time I will live here. The next time I come home to visit, I'll be a visitor." My mother lost it. She wept and cried. She has always been very emotional when it comes to me. I said, "Mom, it's true. I'll be a visitor." And this has held true.

But wherever I've gone, I have always acquired an individual to mother me and support me along the way. I have to take time now to mention just some of those people because it's always nice to tell someone how much you care about them when they can appreciate it. I may not remember all the mothers because there are really a lot of women who nurtured me along the way, but there are quite a few that I have to mention now.

First and foremost is my Godmother, Patricia Smith, who has been an influence in my life since I was fourteen. She has played a pivotal role, not only in my emotional development, but also in my development to knowing the Lord.

One of my other mothers is Yvonne Barnes, my former office administrator for the medical examiner's office in Washington, D.C. She was always there, always caring, always quoting scripture, always keeping calm in the face of adversity. That is Yvonne. I still keep in touch with her and let her know of my progress. She always has a kind, calm word to say. One thing that I learned from Yvonne was to dress for success. Ms. Barnes would come into the office just dressed to the nines every day. We enjoyed the progress that the office was making.

One reason I think I stayed in that office for so long was because she was there.

Another mother that actually I acquired earlier, before Ms. Barnes, was Mrs. Jean Lawson. Mrs. Lawson was a secretary with the Armed Forces Medical Examiner Office, with whom I served for nearly three years prior to moving on to Washington, D.C. She was definitely a mother figure. She was one of the people who kept that area together. She was not a physician, but she was the kind of woman who made you stand up and take notice when she spoke. She didn't play, she wanted it done right, and she had a way of letting even the doctors know that they needed to do the right thing all the time. She would listen to some of our conversations, and she would say to me, "Now look, Ms. Thing, you need to get real, stay real, keep your feet on the ground, and always put God first." We would have some very long conversations about our purpose in life. At that time, I was feeling isolated as the only black physician in my area of the military. She would always say to me, "Now, make sure you have a little fun, and take some time out." I always enjoyed her company. We stay in touch by phone, and when I am in the area on business, I try to visit her. She took me under her wing and taught me how to survive in an old boy's world.

Reverend Judy Talbert is another mother who took me under her wing. This woman lost her son tragically to a familial heart disease problem, and we joined forces to try to make organ donation more equitable to the African-American community. This woman had so much spirit that whenever she called and asked me to do something, I was right there. She was a true woman of God's word. We don't keep in touch very much these days, but I know she is on the job and still very dedicated to the cause of organ and tissue donation.

Of course, there were more who "mothered" me. Doctor Calvin Sampson guided me when I was a medical student and helped form me into a pathology resident from Howard. He is retired now, but I can still count on him for good advice. He was a wonderful influence on me. He is a very patient man, methodical, disciplined person who taught me to look at minute details in making sure surgical pathology was done properly. I always called him Uncle Calvin because of his influence on me.

To those named and unnamed "mothers," THANK YOU for helping me grow.

What Advice Do You Have For Parents?

For parents, I ask that they look at their children and remember how glad they were when they were born. Love children this ways always. Never forget to tell them they are loved. Try to encourage them to be independent and confident in their abilities. By all means, encourage their educational goals as early as possible, particularly parents who are African-American, because there is so much negativity towards our children. I don't know if we ever stop to think how we were influenced by the Tarzan movies where it appeared that only a white male could conquer the jungle. We need to let our children know that they can accomplish all of their goals if they are prepared to take the challenge. We need to let our kids know that they are no different than kids of other ethnic backgrounds. Our children need to know that no matter what we look like on the outside, we are all important and can achieve great goals.

In particular, we need to guide girls toward achieving goals. We need to remember that all of our children aren't bad seeds and that for every child that has committed a crime, there are hundreds who haven't. We need to be mindful of the products that we buy and the television program and movies that we watch that don't show our people or our children in a good light. We can do something about that. A lot of the things that we need, to grow up strong and proud, have to come from the home at a very early age. We need to love our kids enough to discipline them and to set limits so that they, in turn, know how to set limits. No matter what we think of our children, and others' children, they are the future. They will be the leaders. They will be our future teachers, doctors, plumbers, and electricians. We need to let them know that as well. We need to remember to tell our children what is a myth and what is the truth.

We need to look at what they watch on TV. We need to make sure that the media is not sending them a negative message. We need to remind our kids that all of our criminals are not black, all of the people on welfare are not black, and all of the prostitutes on the streets are not black. We need to remind them of our heroes and that our real history is going to have to be handed down generation to generation in the old way, verbally. We need to remind our children that many people died for them so that they have the right to learn, to drink water in a public place, and to live in certain areas. We need to remember this fact as adults, all adults. I believe in the old adage that it takes at least a village or a neighborhood or a community to raise a child. All of these efforts are needed to help a child become an outstanding adult.

Do You Mentor?

I always give a whole-hearted "Yes" to this question. I do mentor. I think it's extremely important when one attains a certain career goal to reach back and show somebody else how to do the same thing. One shouldn't be jealous of a protégé or concerned that she/he might take one's job. The fact is, as a medical examiner, I am overworked. I get calls from all over the country, and I couldn't possibly address all those issues. For me, forensic pathology is a career that one must be introduced to properly. We already have stereotypes in pathology that medical examiner's have hunched backs or are disrespectful and grouchy or that they look like Quincy. A black female medical examiner will not be portrayed correctly on TV. It is very important that mentoring continue.

I spend a great deal of time out in the community so people can see me. I want children to see me and say "I can be like her; I can do what she does." It's a non-hospital-based medical specialty that I just happened to discover because I was interested in the field of science. Had I not been introduced to it correctly, I probably would not have been successful. So it's very important and incumbent, I think, on African-American professionals to go into the community and say, "You can do this." They must also demonstrate *how* it is done.   When I mentor, I like to go all the way back and start very, very early with education in the primary grades.   I run into students all the time who are in high school or in college or recent graduates and they want to go on to medical school, or some other school, but they lack the background.   They didn't get the guidance in school to take the science or literature courses.

I need to digress away from science just a little bit.   I was giving a talk at a job fair at a high school many years ago. A young man said he wanted to go into radio and TV.   After he talked for a while, I said, "You know, you have got to go back to school and learn how to speak correctly.   Learn how to enunciate and how to use grammar. Otherwise, you are not going to make it in advertising and commercial radio if you do not know how to speak correctly."   I did not tell him that in a public, offensive, or disrespectful way.   I was being as honest as I could be and that young man took me seriously.   He thanked me, and about six months after that, he sent me a certificate.   He had gone to night school and had learned how to use the English language properly so he could go on the major job market.   For those who want to get into science, there are prerequisite classes to take to get into college or to get into a pre-med program, then into medical school. When I go back and talk to kids, I want them to know that I did not just hop over a line to become a doctor. Our children must be prepared to deal with pressure. We really have to try to encourage mentoring for students to bolster their confidence. We don't have enough physicians, and I can certainly say that we don't have enough medical examiners. So mentoring is extremely important in order to encourage children to prepare themselves for their careers.

Mentoring also allows me to reach out and touch the community. I realize I have a responsibility since I represent the community. I put a face on the community, and I'm proud of that. I want the community to know that I respect them because, certainly, in a way they mentored me. How did that happen? When I was in college, my undergraduate school was a very small, white Lutheran majority school, and the only black people that I saw were in housekeeping and my classmates. I have always really felt for the housekeeping staff and other blue collar workers, what some people consider menial laborers. These people fulfill a necessary role. I greet these people as individuals with a smile, not as the invisible man, and, let me tell you, I developed some good friendships. I think it's horrible, again, to let people think that you belong to a special club and you can't break out of those walls. You can have friends in all walks of like. They have taught me a thing or two. They had a role. Some people say don't forget people you grew up with. This is also a form of mentoring. That interaction. It's called "keeping it real."

Another way to mentor is to groom people who follow; this is mandatory for the groups' survival. I won't always be in this position, and I certainly won't always exist. I have a limited lifetime just like everybody else. I would like to see this legacy that I have begun continue. I think it is really an honor and a privilege as an African-American to do what I do, to be able to bridge that gap, to realize there are always two families involved when there is a death, particularly, a violent death. I remind the people I mentor that attitude is not found in the textbooks, that attitude comes from experience. That's very important. I believe mentoring is one way of tithing as well, sharing one's knowledge. I ask this question, "If you have knowledge and you don't share it with anybody, do you really have knowledge?"

What Advice Would You Give To Young People Reading This Book?

To young people, I say, "remember who you are, or if you do not, then find out who you are, what you like, and what you want to do. Everybody reading this book or talking to me is not going to become a medical examiner, nor should they. But find something and aim toward it. I don't think there is anything we can dream of that we cannot do, *if* we have the proper background. In all things, education is a *must*! Reading and writing, good communication skills, and math are necessary in every profession, whether it be a lawn care, electronics, or cosmetology. We all need those basic skills.

It is good to admire athletes for their physical prowess, but we need to remember something. If we were all meant to be athletes, there would be no one in the stands to cheer us on. We all have a role to play. Unfortunately, sometimes we are not shown the way or we are led to believe that it's not the right way. We need to be smart about the choices that we make early on because they can affect us later in life. We need to try to enlarge our world whenever we can. The simplest way we can do that is to READ! Please, pick up a book! Start out with comic books, anything, but READ! We have to learn to read and write. Why? Because we need to tell our history. We need to make sure our history continues and that we learn it. That is where information is. We are not going to be able to maneuver around in this society without those basic skills. For young people, male and female, take strength in knowing, as an adult, you can be successful. You first have to believe in yourself.

Beyond believing in yourself, you need to recognize that you have self worth. Don't fall prey to personal pathology. Don't let someone make you think you need to take that drink to be popular, to be sexy, or to be successful. Try to look into why you are being targeted to buy certain products so that you don't waste your energy. Who you are comes from the inside. How you feel about yourself will show on your face. You don't always have to follow the crowd. You need to follow your own mind, and the freedom to follow your own mind comes with the ability to make your own decisions based upon merit.

Unfortunately, we live in a world where we are segregated, separated because of what we look like. I don't know when that will ever change, but it's a new millenium, and I can tell you for a fact that the longer we live, the more changes we are going to go through. That's part of life. If we just settle on outside appearances, that too, in time, will pass. But a strong inside will always be there for support. So please consider this: there is nothing wrong with being different as long as you are not harming somebody else. There is nothing wrong with thinking deep thoughts. There is nothing wrong with being a person of color because you are beautiful and so is your history. You need to know that and believe that.

I wish you luck and success, and I hope that you remember that there are so many things you can do and that it takes all kinds of people to make the world go round.

What is Ebonomics?

A frequently asked question when I speak in the African-American community is "What is Ebonomics?" Ebonomics actually is a term that I developed several years ago; it is a personal commitment to invest my resources, experience, professionalism, and money into the African-American community. I developed this term when the media was carrying on about the term "ebonics." These words do not mean the same thing, and it is not just a matter of pronunciation. I guess the best way to explain it is to tell a story, a true story.

When I was a medical student at Howard University, I had the honor of working with a plastic surgeon. In fact, I believe this was the first, black, board-certified plastic surgeon in the country. I was just elated to be assisting him. We were in the operating room, and he had classical music going, and I was standing against the surgical table, just listening for any pearl of wisdom he might drop my way about career paths and solutions to problems. He said, "I'm going to tell you something." I got ready to catch this bucket of knowledge, and he said something that I have never, ever forgotten. He said,

"Let me give you a word of wisdom. Never have a black accountant."

"What? What do you mean?"

"Never have a black accountant."

"Why?"

"Because they go to a party, get drunk, and talk about your business."

I couldn't believe it. So I said to him, "What if the black accountant said to his family, never get a black plastic surgeon, then you wouldn't have any business." And I started thinking: *If we thought that negatively about each other, we would never get anything done.* But history books reinforce this trend, particularly in the black community. We are so willing to think the worst of our black colleagues and of our black communities. In observing other ethnic communities, I feel they have it right, and we still have a way to go as minority people. We need to work together. Everyone has something to contribute.

Some areas of our society foster the notion that if it's black, it's tainted and not as good, and you can only really stop this attitude from progressing by training young minds and leading by example. I've gone out of my way to find people who look like me, if I could, who had a business that I could use, and to use it. Now, I don't mean to say that everyone black is a wonderful businessperson or has a wonderful product, but we should give them the benefit of the doubt. If we don't start crossing that line, then who will? Look at the Jewish community, for example. They work within their ethnic group, and they have basically eradicated those negative terms that could have been used to depict their faith. As well, look at the Vietnamese ethnic group. They bond together, they work together, they bank, and they then present a unified front. We can learn from that. We can truly learn from that.

Ebonomics is a concept that I try to live. In some ways, I think I have to lead by example. I have to be committed in that. I have to be very practical. I don't have another frame of reference; I am a black woman. I will always be one; I was born that way, so my environment is shaped by my external appearance which is unfortunate, but that's the way it is. I have committed myself to things that are really relevant. I don't have the time for frivolous exploits. I do not watch much TV. I cannot relate to shows on TV that do not have black characters that are playing main roles. First of all, there are very few environments where there is no color in the world. I do not go to see movies that are not relevant to me. I don't feel I should pay money to be entertained when we are not represented. So I don't. I have been committed to that since I was in high school.

I think it's important that African-Americans bond together but not just by thinking that we all have to do the same things. It's very important that our communities are multi-layered and that we reach down or over to link up with somebody else. I think it's a travesty when some black people become professionals, and all of a sudden, they find it distasteful to be among black people. I'm often asked, "What's the key to your success?" Well, part of it is treating people of every walk of life respectfully, treating them the way I would like to be treated. We must accept the different roles people play and recognize that all roles are important. That's how I feel about ebonomics.

As a person who deals with death on a regular basis and the uglier side of life, it's very important to me that I surround myself with beautiful and natural things. I invest in African and African-American art. It's something that I can relate to. I like to be surrounded by vibrant colors, and that is the main type of art that I buy. There is nothing wrong with appreciating the other types, but I'm not generally going to invest in those. Why? Because oftentimes in this country, art that is done by black artists is categorized as black art. It may be of the same quality as the "old masters," but it is categorized differently and therefore separated. So we must, as an ethnic group, bond together and support this work and pull it into the mainstream. It's important that I accept the fact that I want to be taken seriously as a physician. I think other people want to be taken seriously in other professions: plumbers, electricians, yard care service. I feel committed to practicing ebonomics, and I will continue to teach ebonomics for the word. We need to do that. It wouldn't be called ebonomics in another culture but that's what it is - investing and partaking of your own. We need to do more of that.

We have to practice more self-sufficiency so that we have more self-respect in our community. Black people, for a long time, have been described as the consummate consumers. We consume more than we produce. The dollar stays in the black community for such a short time. Some days, the black dollar, and I'm talking about the black dollar from pay check to distribution for consuming goods, may be as short as six minutes or six hours. Why? I point out an example. There are more check cashing stores in the black community and the Hispanic community than in the white and other ethnic communities. The liquor stores that cash pay checks are also in abundance in the black communities. That dollar changes hands right then and there, and we consume goods. That is only going to change if we come together as a group and recognize that.

Another point of ebonomics is embracing and loving our black culture. I would like to see us take on the Jewish practice and eradicate these negative, descriptive terms. The 'N' word is a word I will not say; I will not even read it. Why is it that we don't see slang words associated with other ethnic groups as frequently as we see the 'N' word? Someone has to answer that question. Someone has to be put to task and held accountable for what is going on in our literature, in our audio and visual means of communication. That, to me, defines part of black love. The 'N' word is a negative term that has moved mainstream while other ethnic negative terms are not tolerated. It's up to us to band together as professionals, laborers, and just people in general. It's not acceptable. There is something wrong when we see that word in print, and we don't see other words. Something is very, very wrong. We're not going to see the negative term used against Jewish people in the past that begins with a 'K' in the common media productions. As a matter of fact, if you recall, the artist Michael Jackson used the word in one of his songs and it was taken out. The whole song was re-produced! We need to copy what this group did. It's just not a good thing to allow. Let us teach our children by example.

I become very concerned when young people think nothing of saying, "You know, you're my 'N'." Do they know what that means? That tells me that they're not being taught their history or the nature of that word. People got together just in recent years to put pressure on dictionaries. What do you mean the 'N' word describes a black person? That's a negative term. That only comes about by us banding together and putting some economic pressure on people to make changes.

Another facet of ebonomics is buying, manufacturing, and producing quality products by black people that can be used by the general population For example, within the black culture, we adorn ourselves and want to look good. That is really part of our African heritage. However, we go to the extreme. We don't always do it with the best economic wisdom. As far as marketing concepts go, you will see so many ads tailored to the black community that get us out there to spend money instead of saving it. Or instead of using economic power to support black banks that can re-invest in the community, we distribute our money out into other majority banks that don't always want to invest in our communities. That's part of ebonomics. Black economics is one way of putting it, but it's more than that.

One area that has always disturbed me is this push for our children to wear designer clothes. Some of these designers have been in the media and have stated that they don't want black youths to wear their products. They don't really want to be associated with gangs, and they don't want "common" people to use their products. Yet we still buy them, wear them, and use them. Why not buy from a black group that is producing quality merchandise? I think we, of all ethnic groups in this country, get so mesmerized by labels and names that we forget. It is always disturbing when I see a child who has been shot and killed over a pair of tennis shoes or a similar object. There are very few gym shoes, no matter what their brand name is, that aren't made in Korea for a few dollars, and then the price is added on. It's disturbing that some athletes are willing to put their name on a product that is over priced and is particularly marketed in a black community to people who really can't afford to spend that kind of money on shoes when there are other necessary items they need to purchase. This is a way of selling to people in a subliminal way by saying, "Hey, if you wear this product, this shoe, etc., you will practice and get to the NBA; you'll be rich and famous." That's a problem for me. Common sense is forgotten, and the marketer is simply playing on the consumer's sense of self-worth.

The African-American community must take steps to educate our young people regarding their employment futures. What I mean is that we get really caught up in different types of jobs and then we tend to discredit other types of jobs. Now, it's great to be a physician, but not everyone will become a doctor. We need to be able to service the entire community. When I go to job fairs, it always disturbs me that they don't bring other professional people in who can describe a variety of jobs. It's doctors and lawyers who really predominate the job fairs. That's nice for some people, but there are other necessary, lucrative professions. We tend to disregard professions such as plumbing, electrical work, yard work. The future of this country is resting on computers, so what about learning those skills? My training as a child was whatever I did I should do it to the best of my ability; be proud of it. It's better than not being able to work. In reality, when one does service work, one is in demand and makes money. By applying ebonomics, our young people can see choices in employment. Trade schools need to be supported.

Certainly, doctors don't deliver mail, doctors do not cut yards, and doctors are not going to be called out on a holiday when the refrigerator isn't working. We have to start respecting that it takes all kinds of people to make a world livable. I want to make very sure that we as professionals, especially in the black community, don't get to a level where we think we are better than other people. Our careers, our jobs, and our environments may make us different but they don't make us better than anybody. We have to stop that "Crabs in a barrel" mentality. Attitudes haven't changed that much. If I'm riding in my car and they're looking for a black woman as a suspect, I know I will be pulled over. It doesn't matter what degree I have, I'm going to be judged first on what I look like. We haven't broken those barriers down yet, and that's why we need to strengthen our communities and ourselves. That is my belief and description of ebonomics.

Do You Read Patricia Cornwell Novels?

One question that I encounter rather frequently, particularly when I'm speaking with women's groups is, "Do I read the popular mystery series by the author Patricia Cornwell?" Usually, my very rapid answer is, "No, I do not." But I have to explain. I'm a firm believer that the best way for me to continue to do this job, day in and day out, is to separate my personal life and my professional responsibilities. So I don't find it relaxing to kick off my shoes, throw my tired body on a couch, and pick up a murder mystery. My life *is* a murder mystery, so this would not be all that relaxing. My friends will tell you that I'm just the biggest pain in the neck when I have to watch a movie with them because I can tell them what's going to happen before it happens. I also think it's just a cheap imitation of a type of horror flick murder. I don't find those types of entertainment pleasant or refreshing. There are too many other things I can do for relaxation than to try to replay what I do for a living.

Probably because of the harsh nature of my work, I like to be around natural things. I love putting my hands into the earth and making things grow, and I have a whole green hand. I love nurturing plants back to health, so I surround myself with wonderful green plants in the house, and I have many types of flowering plants in a myriad of colors surrounding my house. I love elements of nature. For that same reason, I surround myself with a lot of wood and earth tones in my home. My friends know my favorite colors are teal and salmon. I decorate my entire home in these shades.

Something else I love to do is to collect African art. I love things that are made by hand and reflect things that are in nature. I love rock formations and I always have a little rock garden around. I love waterfalls, and I have wood carvings from my various travels throughout the world, as well as a large collection of vividly colored, hand woven baskets.

I also love dogs. I have loved dogs from the time I was a very little girl, and I have no fear of animals. Lately, I have participated in rescuing mistreated or unwanted dogs, helping them back to health, and then getting them back to being good natured and socialized. I then let them live with people I know so I can follow up on them. It's like fostering a child. It is really difficult to separate from them once they get used to me, and I get them back to their sweet disposition. I have done that for a number of years, and I currently share my abode with a beautiful little horse that I call Samson who is actually an English Mastiff. Playing with Samson is one of the things I would rather do than to sit and look at a murder mystery on TV.

Personally, I have long-time felt that we glorify violence, and I don't indulge in that. I make sure that I listen to pleasant music, and I like things that I can really learn from instead of having my mind get dull by watching too much silly TV. I like to learn. I enjoy the Animal Planet, the Learning Channel, the Discovery Channel, or places that I can visit in my mind where I have never been before. I find that much, much more relaxing than the "smoking guns."

As much as I like to read, I prefer a good biography because I enjoy learning about people's lives and what influenced them. I have always benefited from that. I still love mythology. I like the world of make-believe where I have to use my imagination. That's probably what I find so irritating about the formula murder mystery. I usually, by the middle of the book, know who did it, why they did it, and how they did it, and that's just not really thrilling for me. But I think we all have different modes of relaxation.

There was a time in my life when I wanted to write the quintessential murder mystery, as I would put it, yet when I began to truly work full-time in forensics, I lost the thrill of that because I feel there is just too much violence in entertainment. I think some of the more provocative murder mystery television shows, movies, and books give sick people sick ideas. I always see a little bit of an increase in crime when a very, very popular type of movie comes out. You see that senseless violent act replayed and that does concern me.

We thrive on violence, too much violence. Most of our popular cartoons contain violence. I feel that in some ways we encourage violence by paying so much attention to it, broadcasting it all over the world repetitively. To me it sends a message to weak-minded people that to be famous, you simply need to commit a violent act. What would happen if we didn't pay so much attention to some of these items? Would some of these copycat shootings we see in schools disappear if we didn't give them the prime-time news coverage, day in and day out? What will happen to children besieged by violent acts from a young age? I watch some of the TV shows, and I wonder who rated them PG? If it's not violence, it's sexual innuendo, and where does it stop? I'm tired of cartoons that show the characters being killed over and over and over again. If a parent or another adult is not there to say, "This is not real," what influence will this violence have in the long run on a child? If it's not the violence, then you've got the cartoon characters that have male and female figures, suggesting that sex appeal will stop a bunny from being chased by a man with a gun. I think we need to look at what we teach our children.

We talk about violence when it occurs in our neighborhoods, but we don't do a whole lot to stop the manufacturing and sale of bullets and guns. That's business. Certainly, our most popular movies are of violent acts. You don't get too many people going to see acts of kindness in movies. I feel that in some way we, as a society, perpetuate violence and then turn around and say, "Gee, our kids are violent." What do we want? What's the cheer we hear at a ball game? Is it "Kill 'em" or just "Push 'em aside." Everything is geared toward violence and it's too much. I just refuse to bring violence into my home. I am glad that the medical novels exist, but not for my relaxation.

Are You Married?

This is another question I am asked, particularly by mixed audiences: young people, the elderly, professionals, and non-professionals. When I discuss what a medical examiner is and what the duties of a chief medical examiner are, I discuss how hard I work and my long hours. So, naturally, people ask, "Are you married?" I rapidly reply, "No." I say I am single, *single and calm*.

Many young people want to know if this is a profession that a woman can do and still be a wife and mother. I wholeheartedly think that a woman can do this whether she is single or married with children. Now, she may not want to be a chief medical examiner; it depends on how much time she wants to put into it. She may want to be an assistant medical examiner. This is potentially a good field for women. Why? One, the hours are more regular than in other types of medical fields. Also, this profession calls for one to be a detail-oriented person. Women are usually very good with details. This job also calls for one to have some sentiment and to be sensitive, and many women are very good at that. In reality, women are the peacekeepers.

I don't want anyone to think that I have given up anything socially to be in this field or at this level. For me, it was a conscious decision. When I was a young person deciding to enter this field, I knew I would remain single for the majority of my life and that has come to pass. I don't think I have given up or done without anything. I have enjoyed a very fun-filled social life, and I feel that, at some point, when it is right, it will be right, and I may no longer be single. I am not waiting or looking for anyone to ride up gallantly on a white horse. While I love to read fairy tales, I know the difference between reality and a good story. If it happens, my mate must be a person with similar qualities: driven, goal-oriented, kind, an animal lover, and a person who enjoys a great deal of time on his own. I don't think it is fair for me to marry and not be very sincere about it.

I know women who have been able to fill all roles: mother, wife, and physician. So don't be discouraged about your marital status. I think it's up to parents to raise strong women and men and to let them know that in some arenas those roles can be interchangeable when it comes to providing a work product. I see the results all too often of individuals who get married or stay together for all the wrong reasons. Likewise, the individual who is unhappy being alone may remain unhappy with another person. Listen to that inner voice. I do. If you are happy and you know it, stomp your feet! Remember that rhyme, "When the right man comes along we will join palm to palm." But until that time arrives, I remain single and calm.

Is There Anything You Would Do Over Again If You Had The Opportunity?

To the young person asking that question, I say a resounding *NO*. Life is too short. If I have made the wrong choice and survived, then I have learned from it. I'm a firm believer in the saying "what doesn't kill you will make you stronger." I must tell you that today I'm a very strong person. Many have tried to slay me, to discourage me from reaching my goal, to put me in my place, and they have failed. And I have become stronger because of it. I think life is too short for regrets. I will have to pick it up tomorrow if I didn't get it today. I look at life differently than most people, I suppose. Experience has been a great teacher. There is really no point in my life that I regret. Although some of my memories are more painful than others, all of this has made me who I am today. This is why cloning people will be problematic. Our experiences help to shape our personalities. I love who I am, I love where I am, and I love where I'm going. I don't have time to think about what I should have, could have, or would have done because there is too much life to be lived in a short time, and no one knows when that time will be up. I try to take advantage of the present. I have heard so many times why it is called the present. It's a gift. Yesterday is gone and will never be again. Tomorrow is not here. There is no time for regrets. There is only time for action.

We dwell too much on the past. We plan too much for the future and let the present get away from us. No regrets! I'm peaceful. I've been through many changes. I have survived many attacks, and I'm all the better for it. Get on with life. If you keep looking back, you will miss where you are stepping, falling into the future and missing out on the present. I know all too well that when time is up; it's up forever.

What Is Your Pet Peeve?

Non-medical people usually ask me this question after I have given a presentation. They are still curious about why I continue to this work. It is amusing to me that the question contains the word "pet" since my enthusiasm for dogs is hard to contain.

Like everyone, I have to contend with things I do not like and hope they will change. I have referred to many situations that I feel should be corrected, such as the media emphasizing deaths of the rich and famous, covert signs of racism that lend a negative tone to the developing young mind, and the need for constant education.

One area of dissatisfaction I have not previously discussed is the topic of respect, not for me, but the lack of respect that I feel the medical community has for the patient population as a whole. It appears to me that we, as physicians, feel that our patients are not intelligent enough to deal with health concerns. Patients can play as great a role in their own healing as the medications prescribed for them. Part of healing is believing that you can be healed, whether it is with medication alone or with a spiritual component. Patients want to be talked to, not at. People need to know why they should take a particular drug *before* they get to the pharmacist. Times have changed, and doctors need to realize that there is as much medical information on the Internet and in popular magazines as there is in the new medical textbooks.

The most frequent complaint I receive when speaking to patient groups and regular citizens, is that the doctors, or other professional healthcare workers, do not listen to their complaints or treat them as though they cannot understand their medical conditions. In my direct role as a forensic pathologist, the families often tie their complaints to the doctor's unwillingness to talk to them after their loved one has died. Family members then become suspicious of the doctor and wonder why he or she did not explain the cause of death to them. This is the number one reason why families refer hospital heath cases to me for review. Perhaps, by refocusing patient care education in medical school, this could be remedied.

Another area of dissatisfaction is the lack of respect people have for themselves and others. I am not overly tactful with this subject. If you love yourself, why put your life at risk by using drugs, drinking and driving, having unprotected sex, or failing to seek medical care when you are sick? We disregard our bodies until often we become critical. I ask people to consider this: If not for yourself, then what about that child you brought into the world? What about that woman who brought you into the world? What about that spouse you pledged to love?

I honestly believe that if we learn to respect ourselves and the world we live in at an early age, the whole concept of healthcare would change.

Is There A Spiritual Component To
How You Feel About Yourself
And Your Chosen Profession?

I don't get this question very often, but I'm always glad when I do. By all means, yes. There is a spiritual component to my life that pre-existed before I decided to become a forensic pathologist. I am a Christian. I have believed in the Doctrine since I was a very small child. The reason I approached forensic pathology without trepidation is based upon my fundamental Christian beliefs, that the soul at death separates from the body, and we are left with a shell. That shell is the body I examine in an effort to tell the story of why that person died. I see no reason to fear that dead body. By all means, we need to respect it, but I don't have a fear about the dead body. For me, it's been a personal calling. I believe it's my talent, a God-given talent. I have been blessed in many ways and, certainly, by obtaining the position of a Chief Medical Examiner. Also, I have traveled and learned other cultures, other beliefs, learned that not everyone in the world is Christian, and those practicing other religious beliefs have many threads in common. Above all, all people have many threads in common other than their external appearances.

I have researched and investigated Native American religion and many of the African religious practices, and they have many things in common that I have incorporated into my personal practices. One is just respecting the earth, the place in which we live, and all things in it. I have a tremendous respect for animals and plants, and even though I am a forensic scientist, I just don't know how I could not believe in a Supreme Being.

While in the military, right on the verge of the Gulf War, I was filled with fear of the unknown. How many young men and women were going to die from this war? As a military officer, I was kept abreast of some of the activities that were planned. I recall one night feeling a tremendous burden of fear, of resentment of the war. I learned of the government's plans to move in the ships and line up the missiles. One tactical move was defeated, and it wasn't by the Iranian Army; it was Mother Nature. The weather was too bad. At that moment I prayed and thought that we must respect nature. We must realize that certain elements are out of our control. I have to believe in something. If I only believed in mankind, where would I be? I see the worst that we have to offer each other, the things that man will do to man. Then in the name of a religious leader, we will call other people savages, i.e., concentration camps, historical crusades, wars in the Middle East. It always overwhelms me. But every morning I wake up, and I pray. I pray for thankfulness, another day, another opportunity to help somebody, and for the opportunity to talk to a friend or a family member. Every day.

I have always appreciated the life I have been given. But this job makes me appreciate that the life I have, I may not have for very long. I don't know that I could do this job without a spiritual component in my life. When I'm faced with adversity, which is at least once a week, if not more often, I'm asked how I stay calm. People who know me recognize the fact that every day I have an angel somewhere on my body that the world can see, usually in the form of a pin. Or I may have a cross, either on a ring or dangling from a pendant chain. People who really know me, and believe as I do, know that no matter what I am wearing, an angel surrounds me. I have believed in angels all my life, since I was a little girl, and I envision one that came to me. I know that wherever I go, many times looking alone, I'm not. When I am silent or thinking, I might be in prayer, praying for strength and wisdom, courage and calmness. When I am asked how I stay calm, that's how I do it. I can only do what I can do, and the rest is in the hands of God. I'm not fearful of saying that. You can call me conservative or whatever, but that knowledge of God and Christ is my daily strength. It allows me to do a postmortem examination, it allows me to get on a plane, and it allows me to face criticism, adversity; it's a shield or cloak.

When I was the Chief Medical Examiner in Washington, D.C., I was about to enter into a deposition. Most of the time, depositions can be very adversarial and stressful.

As I was entering a conference room, one of the attorneys for the opposing side walked up the hallway. She was an elderly black female, and I respectfully said, "Good morning."

"Good morning," she said, staring at me. I thought, *Well, what's wrong?* She just kept looking intently, finally saying, "You're one of us."

My eyes got wide and I said, "What?"

Again she said, "You're one of us."

"What do you mean?"

She pulled open her blouse and showed me that she was wearing a Crucifix. I can tell you believe."

I looked at her and said, "Oh, thank you. I have always believed." We went into the room, and to my amazement, the deposition went smoothly, was not adversarial, and this attorney asked no questions. That's only one example.

But I would like to send a message home to anyone reading this: I have been fortunate to know people with other faiths and other beliefs, whether it be someone from the Nation of Islam, a Jewish person, Hindu, Buddhist, or someone of the Bahi faith. People who believe in a Supreme Being, whoever they describe that entity to be, no matter how different, are generally people who care about others. To me that is the most common thread. They care about others and want people to treat them the way they would like to be treated. It may not be the Ten Commandments, but good deeds, respect, and caring have universal appeal.

I don't think I would be able to arise every day in a good mood and work and see what I see and hear what I hear without faith, without my spirituality intact. For me, long after this profession has concluded, my faith will survive.

Why Did You Leave Washington, D.C.?

This is a difficult question for me to answer. First, I never planned to leave Washington, D.C. Living there had been my childhood goal. Once I decided on forensic pathology, once I learned about Washington, D.C., how it was constructed, how it developed, and how it was a majority black city, I made my goal, for the height of my career, to become the Chief Medical Examiner in the city. When that actually occurred, I was so happy. I was finally where I had always wanted to be during those years of school. Education and training had gotten me exactly what I wanted.

Surprisingly, the way I got into the medical examiner's office in D.C. was a little unusual. I was notified about the position opening while serving as the Deputy Chief Medical Examiner for the Armed Forces. At that time, in the late 1980s, the District of Columbia had been without a consistent chief medical examiner for approximately ten years. They had a doctor in an acting position, and the office was in a severe state of depression. It was a job that no one really wanted. Even I was doubtful about it, but Dr. Davis encouraged me, as I stated earlier. When I got to the office, ready and determined to do my best, there were many pitfalls. The office truly was not funded properly. And by the early 1990s, there was a tremendous homicide rate, primarily involving young black males. In fact, Washington, D.C., was the homicide capital of the world for many years. Despite the homicide rate and fact that it was the nation's capital city, the office was so poorly funded it was hard to get a job done. Fortunately, having been in that area for so many years, having gone to school there, and being determined always to be honest about my work, I did establish great rapport with the citizens, the medical schools, and for the most part, the administrators of the local government. But it was still very difficult to complete that job. Amazingly, I inherited a staff of physicians that weren't willing to pull together and accept my leadership, mainly because I, like them, was black, and that I was female. It was kind of mind boggling in 1992 to deal with professional attitudes, or lack thereof, just because I was a person who was instructing them and directing them in their activities, and I was black, just like them. That was hard to accept. It was hard to deal with someone not wanting to do his or her best for the community. Fighting those odds consumed a lot of energy just to perform death investigations.

My first day in the office in Washington, D.C., I became aware of the fact that the staff were still using rotary phones in 1992. There was such a large discrepancy between the Chief Medical Examiner Department and other departments in district government. It was really remarkable, or should I say disheartening? The Medical Examiner's Office had been placed as an office within the commission of public health, and, for the most part, I begged and pleaded for supplies via a secretary who had no healthcare background. In fact, the only time the office received adequate supplies was when the media was about to do a story on the office. That's what it took! It was ridiculous. It was so hard to deal with the public in a place that was so dirty.

Soon after taking over the office, I applied to have the forensic pathology training program reinstated. A site visit was conducted by the Graduate Studies section of the American Medical Association. They came to the office and said they would reinstate the office under my leadership with a promise that the District of Columbia would properly fund the office. That's why the office had lost its accreditation. There was no commitment there. Although we regained the program, the city lacked commitment. It became very hard for all of the employees, including me, to work in an environment where there was no air conditioning, many times no hot water, and no heat when it was cold. Again, these things would only be fixed when they thought the media was on its way. Very disheartening!

I was brought in initially under the first female mayor of Washington, D.C., and I was very proud to serve under her, but still received very little support. I was committed to the city and the people I knew, and that is what kept me for so long. When Mayor Kelly was defeated and Mayor Marion Barry came back, we all hoped for the best. But that was not to be. Not only was the office given little attention, the whole city was punished by the Federal Government for having re-elected Marion Barry. Funding was abruptly cut off, we couldn't pay bills, vendors could not receive payment, and supplies were in very short order. It was a very miserable time, and yet the homicide rate continued to rise. All we could do at the office was to be very honest with citizens, to be as respectful as we could to the bodies, and to let people know why we were not able to complete cases on time. Through it all, the public was understanding of our shortcomings, considering what we had to work with, but it still became very hard to let citizens know we hadn't completed the most simple tasks.

Prior to the new mayor coming on, I had been able to achieve more automation: a security system, a computer system, and a new dictation system. When the Federal funding was cut back so severely, we couldn't hire people to use the new equipment. With a brand new computer system, we still couldn't get the cases out because I couldn't hire secretaries. It was a vicious circle. I have always sworn to be non-political and neutral, and I will always be that way, but it became more difficult because I could not accept favors, and I had to do what needed to be done no matter what the cost. There was a time when most of the staff in the office was paying out of their pockets to get things done. We bought our own film for cameras and processed it privately just to complete a case.

There were two decisions, or should I say two occurrences, that influenced my decision to leave Washington. I had developed a friendship with another co-worker in the City who remains one of my best friends to this day. Her name is Jan, and she is a psychiatrist, working in mental health. The Mental Health Department had been taken under the court for being non-compliant, basically due to poor funding and mismanagement at the top level. Jan and I would sit together during the policy meetings with the City administrators and just shake our heads in disbelief at what we were hearing. Despite our complaints, very little was getting done to have the programs truly work.

At a board meeting, despite each of us complaining about needing supplies and needing financial support to get our jobs accomplished, we were treated to photographs that had been developed following a trip that the City Fathers had taken to Africa. Beautiful, five by seven photographs depicting the tour through many African nations! At this point I thought to myself, *Something has to give! How is it you get overnight development of these beautiful photographs of a trip to Africa and I cannot get the photographs of the homicide victims of the District of Columbia developed?* There was no fairness. It just didn't make any sense. I thought it was time to start looking for a position where somebody truly wanted quality death investigation performed.

The second set of circumstances that led me finally to seek another position in another location was the way the government dealt with medical issues. In 1995 there was a big tug of war going on in the organ and tissue donation arena. I have always been pro-donation, but I have been pro-donation with public education and accountability to the public if the organ procurement agencies would involve the public a little more in what they do and how they do recovered tissue. There was a consistent need to explain to the public about the costs and the fees and have community-sensitive education advertisement. I became very distressed at a law that was passed in Washington, D.C., that allowed rapid organ recovery to begin at one of the large hospitals without enough justified public education. What it meant was that individuals would learn of their loved one's death and at the same time would learn that, by the way, the hospital had instituted putting in a special fluid to preserve the kidneys for transplantation without even asking the family.

Even though I knew why health professionals wanted to do this, I did not think it was fair to the public because they did not have a good understanding of what was going on. What made it so frustrating was that, despite comments from groups of individuals from the healthcare field, from the community, and from the religious areas who had all protested, this law was passed after secret meetings had taken place between the procurement groups, the hospitals, and the City Council members, who did not really want to hear the down side. It was a very sad day. That's what made me consider, seriously, leaving Washington, D.C. It was a difficult decision.

I had visited my Godparents who were living in Houston, Texas, where I would often go to get away, and as I was leaving in August 1995, I said to them, "It sure would be nice to live here all the time. I always enjoy myself so much here; it's such a pleasant place." Then I said, "Ah, that would never happen." But to my amazement, a national search was begun in September 1995 for the Chief Medical Examiner of Harris County. I decided, what the heck! I threw my hat in the ring and, lo and behold, I got a call one day that somebody was going to come up to Washington, D.C. to meet with me. I was very surprised. A woman from the search committee came to D.C. to interview me. It was in November and quite cold and damp, which is usual for Washington, D.C., at that time of year. This woman from Texas, who had been an assistant to the county judge, met me in my office. It was one of the days when we didn't have heat in the medical examiner's office and it was freezing! All my employees, including me, were walking around wearing our coats and gloves. I sat with her and we talked about the office, my career plans, my thoughts about death investigations, and so many other things. As we sat and talked (we were in the conference room in the D.C. Medical Examiner's Office, and we were sitting with a space heater between us, shivering), I thought to myself, *Now, this is ridiculous, I'll never hear from this person again. Look at what we are trying to do.* I took her on a tour, showing her the half-completed things we had begun but because of a lack of funding could not complete. As she left, I thought, *Well, that chance is blown!* To my amazement, a few weeks later I got another call. I was on the short list.

Well, the rest is history. But I was amazed that when I got close in the decision-making process for Houston, I was hesitant about going. I was hesitant about leaving the area that was so close to my family, my grandmother in particular, and the way of life I had known for so long. I sought another person's counsel, Dr. Calvin Sampson, one of my professors from Howard University. I told him that I didn't really want to leave. I had just finished restoring my house, and I had all these reasons why I couldn't go. He said something to me that I will never forget. He said, "You can't marry your house. There is no reason why you shouldn't go, and grow." That motivated me. I asked my grandmother about going; at that time she was ninety-six. I told her I was concerned about going to Texas, a place where I had never lived, that ideas and values were a little different in Texas, and that I didn't want to leave her. This was in December 1995. She told me that her time had come to go to heaven, that I didn't have to worry about her, that I shouldn't stay in Washington, D.C., because of her because she was not going to be around for me for very much longer. That broke my heart. I was more determined not to leave. I spent a weekend with her, and during that time, I realized that she was right. She was ready to go on. I began to feel a little more comfortable about the process. It is amazing. As that process continued and I was in the midst of the selection, my grandmother died. It was very, very hard on my mother yet I was comfortable, peaceful. I knew that Mama Hart had made up her mind. She had lived a long life. Like a miracle, three days after returning from my grandmother's funeral, I was notified that I had been selected to become the new Chief Medical Examiner in Harris County. By the time I heard that, there were no more qualms; I had to go.

Are You a Real Forensic Pathologist/Medical Examiner?

This is a question that I receive so often, it has become expected. It's used as a conversation piece, usually in a social setting. I'm asked that question because some people want to know my opinion of a case; others simply want me to entertain them. To both kinds of people I must say this, "I am a *real* doctor, a *real* forensic pathologist/medical examiner, and a *real* medical examiner is neutral. My responsibilities are to investigate death objectively, to educate the jury in the courtroom because they are making the decision, under law, about guilt or innocence. It is not the medical examiner's place to form an opinion as to who is guilty and who is innocent. That is not what we are supposed to do. We are, as medical examiners, to be available to both sides, the prosecution and the defense. We are to provide information to families who need to know what happened to their loved ones, but we cannot solve every crime. This is a reality between what a *real* medical examiner does and what Quincy, the TV character, did. I think you know which role I play.

Socially, people often ask me, "Was O. J. guilty? My professional opinion is, I do not know, because I have no opinion. I have learned in my twenty-plus years of learning about forensic science that there are at least three sides to every story. There's his side, there's her side, and there's somewhere in between, the truth we may never attain. I have been asked my opinion on the O. J. Simpson case, largely because I am a black female and a chief medical examiner. I must admit that I sometimes wonder what my life would be like if I had gotten involved in that particular case. The truth be known, I actually was asked to participate in the O. J. Simpson trial. But, unfortunately, I was asked six months into the case, and my obligation at that time was to the citizens of the District of Columbia where I was serving as Chief Medical Examiner.

I received a call at home on New Year's Eve from an attorney involved with the defense of O. J. Simpson. I was amazed that they found my unlisted number, but they did. I had to decline because my obligations lay elsewhere. The question was put to me, "Don't you believe in his innocence? Won't you come join the team?"

I had to reply, "I do not join teams; I'm neutral to the core, and I cannot change my beliefs for one trial no matter how much media coverage it might bring." I also replied, "Unfortunately, I think you are asking me because I'm a black female." The individual said, "Well, we just found out you existed."

I laugh to myself when I think about it now because I replied, "I've been existing all my life and I will exist after this. You will have to find someone else. I cannot shed my philosophy for one case." So, in answer to the question, I stick to my guns. My opinion is that "I have no opinion."

Cases like the O.J. Simpson trial sensationalize death. What about others killed in Los Angeles that same night? What happened to them? Were their deaths any less important? Certainly, nobody should die tragically at the hands of another in that way. Nobody! Unfortunately, in this country, we place so much value on notoriety and wealth. I shudder to think what makes someone's death so much more important than another. People with famous relatives lose their right to grieve privately. To those without famous relatives, it almost seems as though their loved ones just were not important. I think it's sad that our society has moved in this direction. Try as I might, with all the individuals I encounter, I try to let them know that as I am doing each and every case, everyone's death is just as important as the next and will be treated so under my watch. A real medical examiner cannot lose sight of the objective to care about <u>all</u> of the cases.

I try to make a point of educating the people who ask these types of questions. No matter how much public interest there is, it is important to stress that "Quincy" was a media portrayal of my profession. Real medical examiners do exist, and I happen to be one!

Why Won't You Eat Devil's Food Cake?

I think it's really important to let young people, male and female, particularly African-American young people, know that they don't have to buy into negativity. What do I mean by that? My mother and I always laugh because I told her when I was a little girl that I wasn't going to eat any devil's food cake. She laughed and asked, "What are you talking about?"

As a young person who really loved to read, who was very interested in different cultures, I learned very early on that my culture was lost to me. I was separated from it, and it hurt. So I went out of my way to learn about Africa and the Caribbean, about South America, places where people of color lived and lived well. I could see in my young mind what I considered the commercial negativity that was all around and it used to make me feel bad. I could see the subtlety that some people never think about, but I was sensitive to it. I always asked my mother, "Why is this dessert called devil's food cake? What makes it devil's food?" I said, "You know, Mom, I love chocolate cake. I LOVE chocolate cake! But I will not eat devil's food. Why would I eat devil's food? That's evil. That's the devil. Why would I eat that? Why is it that because it's chocolate, it tastes good, and it's a deep, rich brown, that it is called devil's food?" Then I would ask her, "Why is the white cake called angel food?" To me, if I ate devil's food cake, I was obviously on the side of the devil. If I ate angel food, I was on the angel's side. Why do we name food like that?

I looked around and saw so many things that referred to brown or black as evil or bad. That bothered me. You know, there are the pure white doves and the black crows. A crow is rarely seen as a nice, good animal. It's evil, dark, or it's corny, or it has "black" Step-N-Fetch-It characteristics. Black humor! I don't know if people are aware of the power of words.

When I was in high school and about to go to my first prom, I received a gift. It was perfume. It was "White Shoulders." It smelled really good, but I told my mother I could not wear that perfume. You see, I was quite aware at that time in my life that I did not fit into the status quo of beauty. I knew in my wisdom at that age that I would never meet those criteria. For me, I rejected any symbolism that imposed the beauty standard of white America. I refused to embrace it. Because that perfume was named "White Shoulders" and the picture on the bottle was that of a white female, I felt insulted; I would not wear it. As much as I loved the scent, I could not, in good consciousness, wear it. So I sought out a cologne that didn't refer to any color of skin or show any color of skin. But I must say, back in those days, it was kind of difficult. Growing up, I would see pictures in the popular magazines of the world's sexiest man or most beautiful woman, but I didn't see faces of color. I remember being overjoyed to see the first black model on the cover of *Glamour*.

Some people embrace the notion that their nose is too wide, their lips are too full, their hair is too bad, their skin is too dark, and they let that minor difference keep them from feeling good about themselves. I feel like this. God made me in His image. I reflect God's work! I know God didn't make a mistake, and I cannot accept the fact that "different" means better in any category. As I look around now, I still see influences that are so subtle. Some images project that if you are one who is not in what is considered the majority, then you are not popular. I say to young people, fight that! Don't believe the hype. Don't let these images of thin, gaunt, sick looking models trick you into abusing your body. Don't let these images of steroid use make you think you want to turn to drugs to look good. Don't buy the image of attractive, successful looking actors photographed for ads, plying young people and encouraging them to purchase alcohol and tobacco products. This will not bring wealth, successful careers, or the opposite sex.

I wish somebody would do some truth in advertising. I wish somebody would show the inside of a body and dare someone to figure out who had black lungs and who had white lungs. I wish somebody would show a true alcoholic down on his or her luck with no home, no family, no job, no future, and no functioning liver. I wish people would tell the truth. I wish that we would continue to teach our children to be colorblind.

I was very touched just recently when a local TV show did a program where they showed white and black dolls to white and black children and other ethnic groups. I was saddened to see that almost all the little girls, no matter what their ethnic background, preferred the little doll with blond hair and blue eyes. It hurt me deeply. There is still a lot of work to be done. This is not to say that a white doll can't be pretty. Of course it can. But we have to encourage our young people. We have to set the example that black is beautiful, all the way down. The only superior being exists somewhere in the heavens.

In the new century, we need to go a little further. It's time we tell the truth. From my perspective, life is so short and precious. People tend to take so much for granted. What about people who don't have the use of their arms or legs or both? What about the people who don't have hair or those who are scarred forever because it was burned away? They are still people, and they still have something to offer.

As an adult who was blessed to have people tell me the truth, I talked to my elders and listened to the history of civil rights. I also traveled to different countries and saw that, underneath the media broadcasts, people generally want the same thing, no matter what. I wonder what we do now to young people to form those opinions? Television tells us that if we are not rich, we are worthless. We have gotten to the point that if we don't show our whole body in a video, we are worthless. Take off your blinders, I say to young people

In my profession, death is the greatest equalizer of all. It does not respect your age, your intelligence, your neighborhood, or your job. There is not one baby that is born with an ounce of hate. It's all learned. We don't need to describe devil's food cake or angel food because we are all going to the same place, one way or another. This is why we really need to encourage our young people to acquire skills so that we can write real history, so that we can get rid of the myths that will have an impact on somebody someday.

I hope that in my lifetime we will no longer have the need for Black History month. I imagine it will begin to be taught alongside the other history that makes this such a great and diverse country. That will be for our future generations. All I can do is try to help and show the way. I hope others will do the same.

"No, I won't eat devil's food cake, but I sure love chocolate!"

Why Did You Dedicate This Book To Dog Lovers?

I have anticipated this question and the answer is quite simple. I'm a dog lover! Why do I love my dogs? After a hard day at work where I may have had verbal insults or I may not be feeling well or I may be tired, overworked, or exasperated, when I come home, my dogs are always happy to see me. Always. You see, dogs aren't hypocritical. If they don't like you, they are not going to want to be near you. They're not going to fake affection. They give you genuine love, and sometimes at the end of the day that's exactly what I need.

Dogs have always been part of my life. My dogs rapidly transform me from being a doctor to a regular human being. Maybe because of the daily exposure to violence and societal ills, I look forward to the rigors of "doggy maintenance."

I began to participate in dog adoption and rehabilitation while in Washington, D.C., and found it a pleasant diversion from my job-related responsibilities. I enjoy helping dogs find new adoptive homes with caring owners. In fact, I have placed five foster dogs with my staff in Houston.

I truly believe that dog lovers are special people.

Afterword

The process I used in writing this book caused me to look back at my life in a way that I had not done before. I am even more thankful that God had a plan for me, and that so many people loved me. My inner strength grew from the wonderful examples set by individuals who impacted the many phases of my life.

When I began to research the cover photograph, I realized that I was smiling much more in the shots with Samson than I was in my white lab coat. This book is about me, and being with my animals is part of who I am. I am just as passionate about mistreated people as I am about mistreated dogs. At the end of the day, no matter how bad it was, my dogs are there to greet me.

The photo of me in the white coat was taken in front of some lovely African artwork with sayings about unity. This artwork is displayed in my office in Houston, Texas. I was accused of having "black power" slogans in my office that were felt to be militant. Whoever complained did not recognize the beauty of these international Red Cross slogans. As you can see, the need for education is continuous.

Now you know a little about me and my profession. To those interested in learning more about the forensic sciences, I have included the addresses of the major organizations in the Appendix. To those inspired to set goals in other areas, know that there are people out there, like me, who want you to succeed. I wish you luck, fortitude, and inner strength.

I learned from my dear friend, Dr. Edith Irby Jones, that being the first means that you need to fight some battles. My armor is strong and will not be penetrated by weapons of fear, ignorance, and prejudices. Whatever your struggle is, know that someone has faced a similar situation. You will get through it. Believe me: happiness and success lie within each of us. All we have to do is tap our inner strength.

God bless!

Appendix

American Academy of Forensic Sciences

Street Address: 410 North 21st Street, Suite 203

Colorado Springs, CO 80904-2798

(719) 636-1100; Fax: (719) 636-1993

E-Mail: membship@aafs.org

Website: http://www.aafs.org

Mailing Address: P.O. Box 669

Colorado Springs, CO 80901-0669

Anne Warren, Executive Director

National Association of Medical Examiners

Secretariat

1402 South Grand Boulevard

St. Louis, MO 63104

(314) 577-8298, Ext. 2

Fax: (314) 268-5124

E-Mail: settledd@slu.edu

Website: www.thename.org

National Medical Association
1012 10th Street, N.W.
Washington, D.C. 20001
(202) 347-1895; Fax: (202) 842-3293
Website: www.NMAnet.org

For military scholarships and information on the Health Professions Scholarship Program, please contact your local Armed Forces recruiter.

About The Author

- First female to head the Medical Examiner Office in the District of Columbia and Harris County, Texas.
- First Medical Examiner to address the Supreme Court in South Africa.
- First black female Medical Examiner in the United States Air Force.
- First Howard University graduate to become a board certified forensic pathologist.
- First in her family to become a doctor.

Joye M. Carter, M.D., resides in Houston, Texas with her English Mastiffs, Samson and Delila. Chief Medical Examiner for Harris County since 1996, she maintains a demanding and hectic schedule, yet she found the time to write a book. Pursuing her passion for education, she writes a monthly, local newspaper column on healthcare issues. Dr. Carter speaks nationally on youth violence, substance abuse, self-esteem, and topics of healthcare and safety concerns.

Contact Information

If you would like to get information about:

- Keynote speaking
- Ordering her book
- Personal career advice

Please send your questions or requests to:

Joye M. Carter, M.D. - P.O. Box 301063 - Houston, Texas, 77230-1063

Website: www.joyemcarter.com

Email: joyemcartermd@aol.com or
        biblicaldogs@aol.com

♦Order Information♦

Book - $12.95 each or (4) for $40.00

Mail orders: Biblical Dogs, P.O. Box 301063
                       Houston, Texas 77230-1063

Fax orders: 713-842-1339

On-line orders: E-mail: joyemcartermd@aol.com or
                       biblicaldogs@aol.com

Name:_____

Address:_____

City:_____ST_____Zip_____

Ph: ( )_____Fax:( )_____

**Add 8.25% sales tax for Texas residents.

Add $3.00 S/H & $1.00 for each additional book.

Check   Money Order   MasterCard   Visa
                       AMEX

Quantity _____   Price $_____
                            Tax $_____
                            S/H $_____
                            Add'l. $_____
                            Total $_____

Card#_____Exp._____

Signature_____

♦ ♦ ♦

I pray for your success.

Believe in Him and in yourself

and you <u>will</u> succeed!

Joye M. Carter, M.D.

Biblical Dogs™